Anonymous

Chicago

A hand book for strangers & tourists to the city of Chicago. Containing historical retrospect.

Anonymous

Chicago
A hand book for strangers & tourists to the city of Chicago. Containing historical retrospect.

ISBN/EAN: 9783337075545

Printed in Europe, USA, Canada, Australia, Japan

Cover: Foto ©Andreas Hilbeck / pixelio.de

More available books at **www.hansebooks.com**

CHICAGO.

A

HAND BOOK FOR STRANGERS & TOURISTS

TO THE

City of Chicago;

CONTAINING

HISTORICAL RETROSPECT; AN ACCOUNT OF THE RISE AND PROGRESS OF THE CITY; DESCRIPTIONS OF THE PUBLIC BUILDINGS, CHURCHES, SCHOOLS, INSTITUTIONS, AND OBJECTS OF INTEREST, ETC.

A BOOK
INDISPENSABLE TO STRANGERS AND VISITORS.

ILLUSTRATED.

CHICAGO:
HALPIN, HAYES AND MCCLURE, PUBLISHERS,
1869.

Press of Church, Goodman & Donnelley.

Geo. DeLoynes.   Geo. W. Parent.

DeLoynes & Parent,

REAL ESTATE,

152 MADISON ST.,

Room 2,   -   Major Block,

CHICAGO, ILL.

KINZIE'S RESIDENCE.

W. H. PHARH & Co.,

Real Estate

DEALERS

AND

AUCTIONEERS,

115 Dearborn St.,   CHICAGO.

Particular attention paid to sub-dividing and selling property at public and private sale. Will purchase half interest with residents or non-residents and divide proceeds. Money loaned on best real estate security, to net-lenders ten per cent. Taxes paid for non-residents and property attended to.

REFERENCES:

A. C. & O. F. Badger, Bankers, Chicago; Fourth National Bank, Chicago; Geo. S. Coe, President American Exchange Bank, New York; Chas. S. Brown President American National Bank, New York; Jay Cook & Co., Bankers, New York; Nathaniel Harris, President National Atlantic Bank, Boston; N. A. Burroughs, President Ketanning Coal Co., Philadelphia; Allen, Copp & Nisbet, Bankers, St. Louis.

TABLE OF CONTENTS.

                                                             PAGE.

Academy of the Christian Brothers 76
Academy of Sciences... 80
Amusement, places of... 124
Art Galleries.. 142
Artesian Wells...55, 59
Banking in Chicago... 106
Boot and Shoe Manufactures..................................... 160
Boulevards and Parks.. 89
Business Directory... 173
Catholic Library Association.................................... 82
Chamber of Commerce.. 101
Charitable Asylums.. 95
Charitable Eye and Ear Infirmary............................... 100
Charity Dispensary.. 99
Chicago Clearing House... 106
Chicago Library Association..................................... 82
Chicago Medical College... 78
Chicago Theological Seminary 73
Chicago University 71
Churches in Chicago...86, 93
City Dispensary... 99
Commerce of Chicago 26
Crib, The Lake.. 48
Custom House 101
Dearborn Park... 43
Dispensaries 42
Distances on the Pacific Railroad 70
Elevators... 28
Erring Woman's Refuge... 94
Foreign Consuls in Chicago...................................... 84
Garrett Biblical Institute...................................... 74
Grain Trade 28
Hahnemann Medical College....................................... 78
Harbor and River.. 44
Historical Retrospect 19
Historical Society.. 81
Hospitals and Dispensaries...................................... 97
Hotel for Invalids.. 94
Hotels... 134
Industrial School.. 104
Insurance Companies.. 109
Irish Literary Association 82
Jefferson Park.. 43
Lake Marine... 24
Lake Tunnel... 49
Libraries... 81
Lincoln Park.. 89

Table of Contents.

	PAGE.
Literary and Scientific Institutions	80
Lumber Trade	81
Marine Hospital	97
Masonic and Odd Fellows' Guide	133
Medical Colleges	76
New Pier	46
New West, The	63
Newspapers and Publications	85
Observatory	71
Opera House	122
Orphan Asylums	96
Pacific Railroad	63
Parks and Boulevards	89
Places of Amusements	122
Population of Chicago	34
Population of the New West	63
Post Office	101
Provision Trade	29
Public Buildings	101
Ravenswood	165
Reading Rooms	83
Real Estate	22
Reformatory Institutions	94
Restaurants	138
River and Harbor	44
River Tunnels	51
Savings' Banks	107
Schools	78
Slope of the Pacific, The	63
South Side Parks and Boulevards	41
Steamboat and Transportation Companies	84
Stock Yards	56
Suburban Villages	165
Telegraph Companies	83
Territory of the New West	63
Theatres	122
Tonnage of Vessels	24
Trade and Commerce	21
Union Park	42
Union Stock Yards	56
Universities and Colleges	71
Vernon Park	43
Village of Jefferson	170
Washington Heights	167
Washingtonian Home	94
Washington Park	43
Washington Street Tunnel	51
West Side Parks	42
Woodland and Groveland	43

PATENT HINGE TURN-UP SEAT DESKS,
FIVE SIZES.

MANUFACTURERS OF ALL KINDS OF

Office Desks and School Furniture.

CHURCH, HALL,

And LECTURE ROOM SEATING.

Everything pertaining to the Furnishing of Schools, Halls, Churches or Colleges. Cutter's Physiological Charts, Tablets, Cards, Charts and Globes of all kinds. Holbrook and Philosophical Apparatus, Magic Lanterns and Slides.

☞ *Address for Illustrated Catalogue and Prices of each department.*

A. H. ANDREWS & CO., Manufacturers,
111 State Street, CHICAGO.

CHICAGO WATER WORKS.

E. P. DWYER & CO.,

IMPORTERS

AND

WHOLESALE DRUGGISTS,

92 AND 94 LAKE STREET,

CHICAGO, - - - ILLINOIS,

Offer to the Trade one of the largest and most complete stocks to be found in any Drug House west of New York City. An examination of our stock and prices is respectfully invited.

E. P. DWYER & CO.

Acids, Brushes all kinds, Chamois Skins, Corks all kinds, Drugs, Dye Woods, Dye Stuffs, Essential Oils, Glassware, all kinds, Indigoes, all kinds, Japonica, Oils, all kinds, Patent Medicines, Rosins, Sal Soda, Soda-Ash, Soda, Caustic, American; Soda, Caustic, English; Sponges, all kinds, Tieman & Co's Colors, Dry and in Oil, Tilden & Co's Solid and Fluid Extracts, Wm. Tilden & Nephew, Varnishes, J. P. Smith & Sons', Varnishes, Window Glass, White Leads.

Agents for Congress and Empire Spring Co. Saratoga Waters, Getttysburg Water, Missisquoi Water, Parke, Jenning & Co's Fluid Extracts, Norwood's American Isinglass.

The Qualities of the Goods in which we deal will always be of the very best obtainable, and put up neatly and carefully by experienced employees.

We do not employ Traveling Agents, being satisfied Goods can be sold at a lower margin of profit by Customers sending us their orders direct by mail. They may rest assured of getting the benefit of any decline in value of Goods, and prices will be as low as if the purchaser were in market.

HISTORICAL RETROSPECT.

Early in the year 1673 a party of five Frenchmen, under the lead of Louis Joliet, set out from Canada, for the purpose of discovering the source of the Mississippi river. The celebrated French Jesuit, Pére Jacques Marquette accompanied the party as a missionary amongst the Indian tribes. Returning home, after a toilsome and adventurous journey, they took a different route, and touching the shores of Lake Michigan, they entered the mouth of a small creek, which the natives called *Chicagon*. This is the first record we find of Chicago River. In 1795, in a treaty with the Indian tribes inhabiting this part of the country, the United States acquired several tracts of land, among which we find recorded a tract of land "six miles square, at the mouth of Chicago river," which then entered the lake about half a mile south of its present mouth, as described in a subsequent article in this book treating of the river. The first white man who became a permanent settler here was Mr. John Kinzie, an Indian trader, who crossed the lake from St. Joseph, Michigan, in 1804. He was the founder of the commerce of Chicago, which then consisted simply in bartering with the Indians for the furs and peltries which were collected by them in the country bordering the Mississippi and Illinois rivers, carried across the portage between the Illinois and Chicago rivers, and then transmitted east in small vessels. About this time the first fort was erected—a common frontier block-house, which was situated near the site of Rush street bridge, on the south side of the river. Outside the fort Chicago then consisted of but five houses: first, Mr. Kinzie's, on the north side of the river, opposite the fort, and a little west of this the residence of a Frenchman, named Ouilmette, employed by Mr. Kinzie, and still further west, where the railroad depot on North Wells street now stands, the cottage of a discharged soldier named Burns. There was also the agency house or factory, where the goods were stored, and the intercourse with the Indians took place. This building stood west of and outside the fort; south of this again was Mr. Lee's farm.

The Indian tribes who occupied the country around Chicago were the Potawatomies, the Miamies, the Winnebagoes, the Sauks and Foxes, and the Kickapoos. On the 15th of August, 1812, occurred the fearful Indian massacre, which forms such a dark and bloody epoch in the early history of Chicago.

In July, 1815, at a grand congress of the Indian tribes of the Northwest, assembled at Portage des Sioux, on the Mississippi, a treaty of peace was negotiated between them and the United States Government. By another treaty, made in August, 1816, all the region of country lying between the Illinois river and Chicago was ceded to the United States. This was effected, it is said, for the purpose of building a canal to connect Lake Michigan with the Illinois river. Four years after the massacre by the Indians and destruction of the fort the troops returned to the neighborhood, and erected a new fort on the site of the former one. This last remained standing as late as 1857, when it was removed by the city authorities.

In this new fort the troops remained until May, 1823, when the place was left to the care of the Indian agent and several families who had arrived here. In 1828 the fort was again occupied by troops, a second massacre being threatened by the Winnebagoes. In 1832, at the breaking out of the Sauk war, the fort was garrisoned by a detachment of regular troops under command of Gen. Scott. In 1836 the Indians were removed, and the fort had no further need of a garrison. In 1830 Chicago had twelve houses and three suburban residences on Madison street. The population numbered about one hundred souls, including half breed Indians and negroes. August 10th, 1833, the town of Chicago was organized, by the election of five trustees. There were then twenty-eight voters. The town was incorporated as a city March 4th, 1837, and the first municipal election was held May 1st, 1837. On the 1st of July of this year the first official census was taken. Population, 4,170. The city then contained 4 storehouses, 398 dwellings, 29 stores for dry goods and varieties, 5 hardware stores, 3 drug, and 19 grocery and provision stores, 10 taverns, 26 groceries, 17 lawyer's offices, and 5 churches.

The only news of the outside world obtained in those days was by a half-breed Indian, who journeyed on foot, once in two weeks, to Niles, Michigan, for papers and letters, the trip usually consuming a week.

The first Circuit Court was held in 1831. The public expenses of Cook County, which then included Du Page, Lake, McHenry, and Will counties, for the year 1832, were $252.35, and the receipts from licenses and taxes, to pay the same, amounted to $278.28.

Such is a brief outline of the more notable events which marked the early days of Chicago. But little more than sixty years since the first white man made this his home—here, where now the merchant princes of a great metropolis luxuriate in costly marble palaces, and view the waters of Lake Michigan whitened by the argosies of a vast commerce—fifty years ago the savages of the wilderness satisfied their thirst for blood, and exultingly celebrated by the blaze of a burning fort the massacre of its garrison.

TRADE AND COMMERCE.

In 1840 Chicago was a trading post. on the extreme Indian frontier, unknown except as a government post. In 1869 her fame as a great city, unique and unparalled in her progress, is world wide. The history of centuries is comprised in her story, embracing a span of not more than half an ordinary life time. A stranger visiting Chicago, seems to enter into a new world. Here alone he can form some just conception of that almost illimitable territory which lies beyond the great

22   *Trade and Commerce.*

CHAMBER OF COMMERCE.

rivers of the West,— the Ohio, Mississippi and Wisconsin. This immense territory, rapidly filling up with a hardy population, whose labor causes the teeming virgin soil to bring forth abundantly of her inexhaustible wealth, is netted with railways and intersected with canals and water courses, of which Chicago is the *entrepot* and mart; and from whence depart every hour of the day and night vessels innumerable, leviathan propellers, and mammoth trains loaded to their fullest capacity with grain and provisions for eastern ports, to be thence transhipped to Europe

Chicago is the centre of the greatest railway system in the world. Not a section of the great Northwest but is connected with it by rail. The Chicago and Northwestern Railway stretches away to Lake Superior, and with the St. Paul road, bisects Wisconsin, and penetrates Minnesota, tapping the entire railway systems of those States, and striking the line of the Northern Pacific Railway, the Galena division of the same road.

The Chicago, Rock Island and Pacific road, and the Chicago, Burlington and Quincy road respectively, connect with the Iowa railroads, extending into Nebraska, and connect at Omaha with the Union Pacific railroad. The Chicago, Burlington and Quincy road connects also with the Hannibal and St. Joseph road, passing through northern Missouri to St. Joseph, which is connected by rail with Lawrence, Kansas, where another connection is made with a branch of the Union line to the Pacific. These various lines, together with the Chicago, Alton and St. Louis, the Illinois Central, and the Chicago and Milwaukee, constitute the main western lines of railway centering at Chicago, and with their connections, place the entire Northwest under tribute to that city.

The aggregate length of the lines of railway radiating from Chicago, is over 8,000 miles. Besides commanding the trade of the interior by its numerous lines of railways and its water communications by canal with the Illinois river, it is at the head of lake navigation, and has access to the ocean by natural and artificial outlets for vessels that safely cross the Atlantic.

A very short time hence these outlets will be so increased that Chicago will be able to send her marine direct to the ocean *via* the St. Lawrence and Mississippi. In 1836 a few schooners supplied this region with goods from Ohio. Now the lake marine exhibits the following figures:

TONNAGE OF VESSELS

Owned in the District of Chicago, that were engaged in trade during 1867–8:

```
  8 Steamers with..................................  3,181 Tonnage
 18 Propellers  "  ..................................  6,020    "
 83 Tugs        "  ..................................    977    "
 41 Barks       "  ..................................18,899    "
  4 Barges      "  ..................................  1,934    "
 15 Brigs       "  ..................................  3,500    "
257 Schooners   "  ..................................43,968    "
 87 Scows       "  ..................................  2,934    "
  2 Sloops      "  ..................................     16    "
                                                      ───────
410 Total       "  ..................................76,369    "
227 Canal boats with ................................19,784    "
                                                      ───────
                                                      96,153    "
 26 Vessels lost during the year ....................  3,640    "
                                                      ───────
                                                      92,513    "
```

TONNAGE OF VESSELS

Owned in other Districts of the United States, that came to the Port of Chicago during 1867–8:

```
  2 Steamers with..................................  2,190 Tonnage
 74 Propellers  "  ..................................51,053    "
 14 Tugs        "  ..................................    910    "
 90 Barks       "  ..................................28,155    "
 21 Brigs       "  ..................................  5,504    "
395 Schooners   "  ..................................85,648    "
 31 Scows       "  ..................................  2,748    "
  1 Barge       "  ..................................    814    "
                                                      ───────
628 Vessels     "  .................................176,511
```

The number of foreign vessels that arrived at the port of Chicago, including two from Liverpool, England, was as follows:

```
  8 Propellers................................... 2,859 Tons.
 26 Barks........................................ 8,308
  2 Brigs........................................   574
 22 Schooners.................................... 5,350
                                                  ──────
 58 Vessels .....................................17,091 Tons.
```

Trade and Commerce. 25

Whole number of vessels and their tonnage which entered the port of Chicago during 1867, compared with 1866:

Number of seagoing Vessels entered Chicago during 1866	997	251,077 Tons.
Number of Canal Boats owned in Chicago Dec. 31, 1866	230	20,059 "
Total number which entered Chicago in 1866 engaged in trade	1,227	271,163 Tons.
Total number in 1867	1,323	289,665 "
Gain in 1867	96	18,629 Tons.

During the year 1867 there were received for tolls on the Illinois and Michigan Canal, $113,482 29.

DIRECT SHIPMENTS FROM CHICAGO TO LIVERPOOL.

The shipments from Chicago to Liverpool direct for the season of 1867-8, were more than double the preceding season. There were forwarded by Webster's European Express, *via* New York, 9,446 packages of provisions, weighing 1,675 tons; and *via* Portland, 13,512 packages, weighing 2,954 tons,—in all, 22,958 packages, weighing 4,619 tons.

The area of the lakes, including Georgian Bay, in square miles, is nearly, if not quite equal to the Mediterranean, while the whole extent of the coast, taking in the St. Lawrence, is far greater. The shore line of the lakes is estimated at 6,240 miles.

If we cast our eyes over the map of the Mediterranean, we are equally surprised to perceive, whether from the difference of institutions, governments, or peoples, that notwithstanding the antiquity of its advantages, so to speak, there is but one port which is as flourishing as Chicago, and none which has risen so rapidly or is likely to advance so far.

Marseilles is the third city in France, ranking next to Paris and Lyons. According to the most recent accounts, its population is, even now, but about thirty thousand more than that of Chicago, if even that; though Marseilles existed six hundred years before the Christian era, and was a free commercial city in the year 1226. The tonnage of French vessels now engaged in its foreign trade appears from our latest Consular returns to be but 180,000 tons; while that of Chicago, as we have already stated, amounts to 255,000. So, too, of Genoa, the proud, the great port of Italy. This city, old and beautifully picturesque though it be, has not as many inhabitants as Chicago, and no such commercial activity. The operations of a single hour in the latter would, in Genoa, appear like an insurrection. And so we might proceed to contrast every other city on the shores of the Mediterranean, all old and flourishing, perhaps, in the European sense, but none of them resembling the busy, growing, flourishing and commanding city of Chicago.

The prosperity of its inhabitants has proceeded step by step with that of the city, and nowhere can be found more of the comforts and elegancies of life, nowhere a greater liberality of bestowment for any good and patriotic purpose.

But it is sufficient for us at this time to look at Chicago as she is, with interminable lines of railway, which reach to the Gulf of Mexico and the Atlantic, with a uniform guage, radiating in all directions over our fertile Western plains and prairies, and which, after cutting through rocks sparkling with gold and silver, are to terminate only on the shores of the Pacific. It is sufficient to consider that she is the mistress and at the head of navigation of the largest inland seas on this continent, and that her sails whiten and her screws toss into foam the purest and most beautiful of waters. With a vast domestic and increasing colonial trade, likely to be facilitated by the enlargement of the present canals of Canada, or the construction of new ones by natural routes such as the earliest missionaries discovered, there seems to be no limitation to her extension or prosperity. Chicago, therefore, may be set up as a standard American city, for the admiration of the world.

THE COMMERCE OF CHICAGO.

THE GRAIN TRADE.

By far the most interesting and remarkable feature of the business of Chicago is the grain trade, which,

Trade and Commerce. 27

starting up a little more than twenty-seven years ago, has developed with such rapidity, and has already reached proportions so gigantic as to stamp it as one of the chief marvels of the history of modern commerce. Who, dating back to 1838, when the sum total of the grain trade of Chicago was *seventy-eight bushels*, could have realized the marvel that thirty years would produce. Then, the only trade of the city was supplied by two small vessels; now, Chicago estimates the tonnage of her fleets by thousands, and takes rank as the leading grain market of the world. The trade and commerce of the Mississippi river has not kept pace with the development of the country through which it runs, and for which it is the regular channel to the ocean. The artificial highways of trade, canals and railroads, have tapped the West, and carried its products eastward across the continent. The grain trade of the West has been diverted almost entirely to the lakes, the Erie canal, the St. Lawrence river, or the six great trunk lines of railroad that diverge from the heart of the West to the seaboard. Thus has the Mississippi ceased to be the outlet to the ocean for the grain traffic of the West. The reasons for the change are apparent, its advantages many. The risk of damage to grain or flour, which was very liable to receive damage from heat by passing through the Southern latitudes of the gulf during the summer months, is greatly decreased, and the uncertainty of river navigation is removed, while the advantages of cheaper and speedier transportation by railroads and canals on the Northern route, with the better markets afforded on the Atlantic seaboard, have aided chiefly to effect this change.

The following figures, compiled from the official report of Chicago Board of Trade, will afford the stranger some idea of the extent of the grain trade of Chicago.

THE ELEVATORS.

Overhanging the river on either side are to be seen large, sombre, gloomy-looking buildings, erected for the purpose of receiving and discharging the enormous quantities of grain which are continually pouring into this market. Their number and capacity are as follows:

Trade and Commerce.

WAREHOUSES.	Receive from	Capacity.
J. E. Buckingham & Co., A	Illinois Central Railroad and Canal	700,000
J. E. Buckingham & Co., B	Illinois Central Railroad and Canal	700,000
Flint, Thompson & Co., A	Chicago and Rock Island Railroad	750,000
Flint, Thompson & Co., B	Chicago and Rock Island Railroad	1,250,000
Munn & Scott, City Elevator	Railroads and Canal	1,250,000
Munn & Scott, Union Elevator	Chicago and Alton Railroad and Canal	700,000
Munn & Scott, North-Western Elevator	Chicago and Alton Railroad and Canal	600,000
Munn & Scott, Munn & Scott	Chicago and North-Western Railroad and Canal	200,000
Armour, Dole & Co., A	Chicago, Burlington and Quincy Railroad	1,250,000
Armour, Dole & Co., B	Chicago, Burlington and Quincy Railroad	850,000
Munger & Armour } Consolidated into { Munger, Wheeler & Co.	Galena and Chicago Union Railroad and Canal	600,000
Hiram Wheeler	Galena and Chicago Union Railroad and Canal	500,000
Galena Elevator	Galena and Chicago Union Railroad and Canal	500,000
W. H. Lunt, Iowa Elevator	Canal	800,000
O. Lunt & Bro	Canal	80,000
Finlay & Rogers, Illinois River Elevator	Railroads and Canal	200,000
Vincent, Nelson & Co., National Elevator	Railroads and Canal	250,000
Total bushels		10,650,000

Trade and Commerce.

The following table shows the movements of flour and grain during 1868 as compared with 1858.

RECEIVED.

	1868.	1858.
Flour in barrels	1,821,205	662,540
Wheat in bushels	13,980,857	9,639,614
Corn "	26,136,256	8,252,641
Oats "	13,554,827	2,888,597
Rye "	1,400,896	71,012
Barley "	2,484,450	418,812

FORWARDED.

Flour in barrels	2,246,280	470,462
Wheat in bushels	12,950,293	8,850,257
Corn "	23,062,529	7.726,264
Oats "	12,425,950	1,519,066
Rye "	1,864,566	7,569
Barley "	2;485,959	182,020

THE PROVISION TRADE.

The provision trade of Chicago dates its commencement from the year 1835, when 5,000 head of cattle was the total number cut and packed in the city. From that time until the season of 1864-5, Chicago furnished almost one-third of the entire number packed in the western states. Cincinnati, for a number of years, was the leading packing point, and was, in consequence, called the Porkopolis of the country. In 1861, although Cincinnati showed no considerable decrease in the number of hogs packed, still she had to yield the palm to her younger competitor. During that season nearly one million hogs were cut up and packed in Chicago, being two fifths of the entire packing of the west. The number of firms now engaged in packing is forty-six in pork, and nine in beef. The following table gives the receipts and shipments of hogs, with the number packed in a series of years:

Year.	Received.	Shipped.	Packed.
1832			838
1833			1,000
1834			1,400
1835			5,000
1837			12,000
1851-2			22,036
1852-3	65,158		44,156
1853-4	73,980		52,849
1854-5	138,515	54,156	78,694

Trade and Commerce.

Year.	Received.	Shipped.	Packed.
1855-6	308,539	170,381	80,380
1856-7	220,702	103,074	74,000
1857-8	214,223	88,546	99,262
1858	540,486	192,013	179,684
1859	271,204	110,246	151,339
1860	392,864	227,164	271,805
1861	675,902	259,094	505,691
1862	1,848,890	491,135	970,264
1863	1,677,757	856,485	904,659
1864-5	1,410,320	536,437	760,514
1865-6	1,178,882	662,566	507,855
1866-7	1,341,656	672,769	639,332
1867-8	1,883,873	1,033,118	706,225
1868-9	1,997,506	1,181,844	697,954

The following shows the numbers of live stock received by railroad during the season of 1868 as compared with that of 1867:

	1868.	1867.
Beef cattle	324,624	334,188
Hogs	1,705,868	1,696,748
Sheep	270,875	179,888

The following table shows the result of the packing business in the west during the season of 1868-9 compared with that of 1867-8:

	1867-8.	1868-9.
Ohio	562,955	544,657
Illinois	1,068,496	806,088
Indiana	321,888	326,658
Kentucky	157,880	183,426
Missouri	383,011	361,067
Wisconsin	174,958	129,094
Iowa	182,944	126,835
Total	2,793,832	2,477,264
	2,477,264	
Decrease	316,768	

The packing-houses of Chicago are mainly located in Bridgeport, on both banks of the south branch of the river. The buildings are mainly substantial brick structures. Steam machinery now performs much of the labor formerly done by hand. It is a curious and instructive scene to witness the operations of a large packing-house during the busy season, and will repay the trouble and time spent.

THE LUMBER TRADE.

Chicago is admirably situated for a first-class lumber market for the people of the Northwest. The lumber regions of Canada, Michigan and Wisconsin, inexhaustible as it would seem, are all accessible to the lakes, and lumber is readily transported hither at a trifling expense, so that, in purchasing here, dealers can do almost as well as if in the very heart of the lumber region, many miles distant. The lumber trade of Chicago ranks next in importance to the grain trade, and continues to make gigantic strides each succeeding year, keeping pace with the growth of the city and the development of the Northwest. The receipts of lumber for the fiscal year ending March 31, 1868, were 882,661,770 feet, against 730,057,168 feet for the year previous. The shipments were 518,973,354 feet. The receipts of shingles were 447,039,275, and the shipments 480,930,500. The increase in the latter over the former can in part be attributed to the fact that there is a large number of shingle factories in our city. These, in a great measure, help to meet the pressing demand from all parts of the south and west. The receipts of lath were 146,846,280, and the shipments 70,587,194.

MISCELLANEOUS.

	Receipts.	Shipments.
Seeds, lbs	23,962,397	19,058,921
Salt, bbls	492,129	455,740
Salt, sacks	21,081	8,263
Hides, lbs	28,522,066	27,789,099
Highwines, gals	1,458,228	
Lead, lbs	11,236,957	4,162,077
Wool, lbs	11,218,999	11,293,717

32   Trade and Commerce.

CHICAGO HARBOR.

REAL ESTATE.

ACCORDING to the estimate of many, even citizens of Chicago, whom the experience of the past should have taught better, every advance in real estate has been set down as the result of artificial inflation. Always, a reaction was about to set in and a fall in prices that must surely prove ruinous to the unlucky wight who should have the boldness to base his speculations, in the purchase of real estate, upon his faith in the future greatness of a city, the heart of which was planted in a swamp on the banks of a sluggish stream whose mouth was barred by an ever-increasing sand-bank. The poor laborer who, in the early days of the city, was compelled to receive a portion of his hard-earned dole in city lots, was an object of commiseration. And even to this day we find croakers who, when a man of moderate means stints and saves to enable him, by the expenditure of his last dollar, to make his first payment on a lot, hold him up as a marvel of blind folly. Still, these transactions have gone on, and hundreds of instances can be pointed out to-day in which poor men who had perforce to take lots in part payment of their earnings in despite of themselves, have suddenly awakened to the fact that those same lots, so sadly despised, and the cause of so much commiseration to their owners, have made them independently rich.

Our building enterprises also come in for a full measure of censure from the same class of people. The five to six thousand neat frame dwellings which every year add so many comfortable and pleasant-looking homes for the laborer, mechanic, and man of small means, are looked upon as the mushroom sprouts of a spurious and unhealthy growth ; while such magnificent edifices as are rapidly covering the whole business section of the city as altogether too extravagant — too far in advance of the times, and sure to result in utter ruin to their projectors, and hasten the return of the dreaded "crash" or "crisis." But the work still goes on; no sooner is it announced that another grand "block" or "building" is to be erected in such a place than the architect's office is besieged, and usually before the foundations are laid every choice place in the building is leased in advance. At no time in the history of Chicago have rents been firmer than during the renting season of 1869. A certain evidence of healthy, vigorous growth is that the business portion of the city is rapidly extending, not changing, its location.

Within the memory of men yet living in our midst, Chicago was a mere trading post on the extreme Indian frontier. So late as 1840, the population was less than 5,000, and this memorable year of 1869 it is estimated to be considerably over 300,000. Why attempt to scan the future? The past has realized more than her most sanguine prophet ever dreamed Looking back at what Chicago was in her early days, and comparing her with other and older cities, we may well wonder at her progress; but if we but look a little deeper into the matter, and seek out the true causes of her wondrous and unprecedented growth, surprise at the reality gives place to almost wonder that it is not greater. For, lying behind the great FACT of the city, are greater facts which justify an expectation beyond what the most sagacious or sanguine have indulged. These,— numerous to consider in detail, and fortunately too familiar and obvious to be more than suggested,—are all to be referred, first, to the extent and richness of the region which the city immediately subsidizes; secondly, to the relations between it and more remote lands and interests. "Chicago can scarcely be called a great city, in fact, yet,—only a little over a quarter of a million inhabitants; and he who only estimates the resources of Illinois alone must see that they are more than enough, and are sufficiently tributary to Chicago to secure her present *status* forever. The proposed Northern Pacific Railroad is no less a Chicago interest than are the Union or Central Pacific to be. The freshest tyro in Lake Superior topography knows that the talk about eastern railway outlets in that direction is the sheerest nonsense. Whatever of trade from those vast regions north of the latitude of Chicago does not reach

Real Estate. 35

eastern markets by vessel, must infallibly come here, while the lake marine engaged therein will more and more be owned and controlled here. There is nothing disastrous to Chicago pretensions in the Northern Pacific Railroad scheme, and if there were, the danger would be little imminent in view of the *status* of the Pacific road already built."

The project of a ship canal across the Isthmus of Darien, which, if successful, would, no doubt, divert commerce from the Chicago trans-continental railway line, has been demonstrated to be wholly impracticable short of, at least, twenty years, and in view of the completion of the Pacific road, there is no demand for Mr. Seward's pet project. But, even if built, it would be available only for steamers, inasmuch, as sailing vessels would have to be towed to and from a point two hundred miles at sea, through a region of perpetual calms, or light baffling winds, before reaching the track of north-east and south-west trade winds. They could go round Cape Horn, as they do now, far more profitably, taking into consideration the canal toll, the cost of tonnage, and the increased insurance premiums over rates chargeable on vessels keeping in the open sea.

In the recent strife between the great track lines penetrating from the seaboard to the interior in which each has sought to secure to itself advantages over the other in its connection with the vast railway system of Chicago; Chicago was declared to be the real objective point of the contest. The traffic of the great West — of the rapidly developing regions beyond the Mississippi valley and beyond the backbone of the Continent, even of the Pacific Ocean and of Asia — was the prize; and Chicago, being " the concentrating point of all that vast traffic," (*vide New York Times*,) became the goal which it was necessary to win. Without that the New York and Erie Railroad can not compete for the Pacific trade with either of its powerful rivals, the New York Central or the Pennsylvania Central. With that the three grand trunk lines will stand on a footing of equal advantage. " This contest being decided in the common interest of all, the next struggle," says the *New York Tribune*, "will be for the control of the lines from Chicago to Omaha."

The North-western, and the Chicago, Rock Island and Pacific, and the Chicago, Burlington and Quincy roads have completed their lines from Chicago to Omaha; so that there are three independent lines in operation from the seaboard, through Chicago, connecting with the Union Pacific road to San Francisco.

Not less full of promise to Chicago is the Kansas system of railroads, enjoying common connection with Chicago at Leavenworth. Through this, the best region of New Mexico and Texas will be brought to our door.

Say that all this growth and activity — so varied, so intense, so far-reaching, so hopeful and determined which constitute Chicago, are past finding out in their remote cause; say that a metropolis so entirely out of what might have been expected to be the true course of trans-Mississippi commerce from seaboard to seaboard, was ostensibly improbable. Yet, how far more improbable now — that a great, growing, wealthy, vigorous and ambitious metropolis once built here, productive capital once accumulated and utilized here, a dozen great and extending railroad lines once concentrated here from East, North, West, and South — that such a change as some anticipate, indeed that any change for the worse, should take place within our century in the center and current of enterprise once established at so great cost, and founded deep in the harmony of so many vast, distinct and otherwise conflicting interests. Consider alone the railroad business; throw out of the problem altogether all others — stock, grain, etc., equally commanding; and reflect what concern the old roads, which are constantly expending their incomes in increasing their facilities, and the new roads which at immense cost are incessantly pushing into new fields and subordinating them, have in the perpetuity of arrangements, whose solidest motive lies thus far almost solely in the future. That these vital connections with surrounding commonwealths once exist, is the strongest possible reason why they should continue to exist. Hard-earned capital, dear-bought commercial experience   ringing to their aid sciences laboriously built up and arts patiently mastered—are never Quixotic. The cost will be ever counted of expending millions in first establishing channels of trade, and then thousands of millions in directing it therefrom. Simply because it is cheaper and surer to employ existing channels than to construct new ones, the old ones will be employed; and capital seeking investment will find it in existing enterprises, in preference to expending itself on the superfluous and problematical. The only necessity that can lead to the opening of new lines will be that which lies in the fact that existing lines have become inadequate to the increased demand; and in that fact we find the very promise of Chicago's permanent greatness, in which her citizens have an abiding faith, and which is now stimulating capital to seek investment here. We say "investment" generally; for in this respect the real estate "movement," as it is called, is but the complement of an activity which extends not alone to commerce, but embraces manufacturing enterprise, and the growth of the arts, useful and ornamental as well. The expenditure of eight or ten millions annually in building, and the ten or twelve millions of real estate transfers, in which from fifty to seventy-five millions of dollars annually change hands, constitute a fact too great to be considered as standing by itself. It has its meaning in facts equally momentous and imposing. In this connection it is worth while to note the prevailing fact in regard to Chicago real estate, that this "movement" has been identical with that of the city in population, industry and commercial importance; in all of which, carrying real estate along with it, there has, upon the whole, been very decided progress from decade to decade. Of the two or three periods of depression that have been experienced, not one has extended to five years. As with the ocean, there has been recession here and there, and now and then; but these have been in the nature of an ebb in the tide, which to those who have had faith and pluck enough to take it, has soon proved a flood tide, and borne them on to fortune.

The particular explanation of this is found in the even pace which building enterprise and real estate activity have uniformly kept. For instance, on the removal of Camp Douglas, the ground of that and adjoining localities was subdivided and sold. Prominent among these was the Grove property, and the Wentworth tract,—about four and two years ago respectively. The former was held at $35 per foot, the latter at from $30 to $50. The price seemed high at the time, but the easy terms reconciled purchasers to it. But those who bought only in the expectation of taking advantage of the long time and paying for their lots, were astonished at finding them, within a year, doubled in value. The reason is plain: the ground was near, improvements began on every hand; and now the few choice lots in these tracts which can be had at all, readily command from three to four times the price paid for them. The same thing has been repeated scores of times, and most notably so in the North Division around Lincoln Park; and previously in the West Division around Union Park. There has been no special effort made in these cases by dealers, beyond regular advertising and the brisk competition of auction sales, to increase this activity. It is simply a fact in the normal growth of a city that has grown because grow it must. The average number of new buildings erected in 1868 was about 7,000, at a cost of about $14,000,000. In Colbert's Chicago, we find the following items: "The list" viz.: 7,000 new buildings, "includes more costly buildings than that of any former year, but the number of smaller residences erected is much less in proportion. It is not possible to tabulate the improvements of the year with accuracy at this writing, but we are able to count 12 churches, and about 40 blocks of fine buildings to be credited to 1868, of which 30 will average $100,000 each and one will cost $300,000."

The whole movement, land and building, finds a parallel only in that which has been going on in New York during the same period. It is a movement of the residence population up town and out to the suburbs to make room for improved and stately blocks of buildings to accommodate the annual increase in the business of the city.

It is to be remarked in this connection, that the only cities in which the real estate business can properly be termed a "movement," are the terminal points on the grand central *entrepot* of the Pacific Road and the Eastern connections,—New York, San Francisco and Chicago. Take Cincinnati for example. The sales for the week ending March 5th, numbered but 69, with an aggregate of $257,779.89, compared with 269 sales in Chicago, to the amount of $1,198,859, showing 300 per cent. greater activity here than in Cincinnati. During the month of January the sales in San Francisco, including both city and county, were 492, for an aggregate value of $2,716,823.

The movement here rivals that of New York—the number of transfers in Chicago during the three last weeks of February were 241, 272, and 240, compared with 238, 231, and 173 in New York. On March 10th there were 38 sales in New York, having an aggregate value of $685,000. On the Saturday previous there were in Chicago 32 sales, amounting to $578,000.

It is estimated that there has been attracted to Chicago for direct investment in real estate during the past year alone, at least seven millions of dollars, to say nothing of the amount which has been loaned on real estate securities and invested in improvements.

PARKS AND BOULEVARDS.

LINCOLN PARK.

This Park is situated in North Chicago, on the lake shore, about two miles north of the river. It is bounded on the south by the old city cemetery. Until the present session of the legislature this park covered an area of about sixty acres; additions have been made, or the city has obtained legislative authority for such additions, which will make the park to contain about two hundred acres. For the past three years the city has been employed leisurely in improving the park, and has expended upon it nearly $75,000. This Park, with the exception of Union Park in the West Division, is the only public improvement worthy of the name in the city. The natural configuration of this park is perhaps better than can be found any where else in the vicinity of the city. It is composed chiefly of sand hills, with little valleys and ponds between them. The great difficulty in applying to it the rules of landscape is to obtain black and tenacious earth sufficient to form a proper surface upon which shrubbery and trees may be expected to live and thrive; but this latter obstacle has been removed by the legislature in its recent bill, which has permitted the addition of a large number of acres to this Park on the north.

The boundaries of Lincoln Park are—on the south, North avenue, from Clark street to the Lake; on the west, Clark street to Franklin; thence north on Franklin street to its intersection with the old lake shore ditch, and thence along this ditch to Fullerton avenue; west on Fullerton avenue to a point five hundred feet east of North Clark street; thence north-west, on a line parallel to and five hundred feet east of Clark street, to the centre line of section 28; thence east to the Lake.

About two and one-half miles of drives are already in existence, and the Park has a large number of trees growing within its enclosure. During last summer a series of out-door concerts were inaugurated, which appeared to be the source of much enjoyment.

This Park enjoys one other advantage, which no other Park in the city can enjoy. All the lake commerce of Chicago, represented by its thousands of sail vessels and its steamers, must pass along its front. Scarcely an hour occurs in the summer when there may not be seen what would seem to be an endless line of vessels.

Lincoln Park is at present the most central of any of our urban parks. As has been stated, it is but two miles from the river, while South Park is from five to eight miles, and West Park can hardly be less than four miles from the Court House. To reach Lincoln Park, however, the people have yet no means of railroad transit except the horse cars, and it will be found that the

South and West Parks can as quickly and as cheaply be reached by the steam roads as Lincoln Park can by means of the horse cars

The lake shore drive or boulevard, which is projected for this Park, will, when it is completed, be one of the finest improvements in the city. The design is to have it commence at Pine street, and run thence along the lake shore, of a width of two hundred feet, until it reaches the southern boundary of Lincoln Park. The Board of Public Works has already matured the plans for this work, and its execution will be only a matter of time.

THE SOUTH SIDE PARKS AND BOULEVARDS.

There are two parks,—one of them containing about 600 acres, and skirting the lake shore just south of Hyde Park; and the other, of 360 acres, approaching nearer to the city, and bounded by Fifty-first street on the north, Sixtieth street on the south, Kankakee avenue on the west, and Cottage Grove avenue on the east. These Parks are connected with a Boulevard 600 feet wide, lying between Fifty-ninth and Sixtieth streets, and all together is called the South Side Park. The northern or western one, or portion of these Parks, is approached from the city by two boulevards or avenues,—each two hundred feet wide,—one beginning at Thirty-fifth street, or Douglas place (the streets are numbered from the river southward), and lying west of the east line of Kankakee avenue, running directly south to the north-west corner of the Park; and the other commencing at the city limits, at Fortieth street and Cottage Grove avenue, running thence in a southeasterly direction to Forty-first street; thence south along Drexel avenue to the north-east corner of the Park, as shown by the map. The Park bill became a law by the action of the last Legislature (1869), and a vote of the people of more than two to one in favor of the Park.

The Commissioners are men of unbounded energy and perseverance. They have already organized, and begun to prepare plans for laying out and improving these Parks, for which purpose ample provision has been made, both in the Park bill itself, and in the Lake Shore Harbor bill, recently become a law by the action of the Legislature.

So that when, a very few years hence, these grand Parks and Boulevards are fully completed, together with all the avenues leading thereto, Chicago will have the finest drives and most beautiful public grounds of any city on this continent.

THE WEST SIDE PARKS.

The West Parks have been left indefinite both in respect of size and exact location. They are to be three in number, and are to be situated within the new city limits, which are extended two miles west of Western avenue: one north of Division street; another, between Kinzie and Harrison streets; and a third, between Harrison street and the Chicago, Burlington and Quincy Railroad. They are each to contain not less than one hundred acres nor more than two hundred, and are severally to cost, improvements not included, not more than $250,000. Wide boulevards will connect the parks with each other, and extend southwardly from the most southern park to the Illinois and Michigan Canal, provided that the land therefor shall be obtained free of cost. When these parks shall have been located, the city limits will be extended so as to include them with all the intervening land between them and Western avenue, and the vote that ratifies the park also extends the city limits.

UNION PARK,

In the West Division, contains about sixteen acres. It is of an irregular, pentagonal form, bounded on the north by Lake street, on the south by Warren street, on the west by Reuben street, on the north-east by Bryan place, and on the south-east by South western avenue. The costly plan of improvement commenced in 1865 is rapidly transforming the flat, bare prairie into a tasteful, beautiful park, with hills, rocks. rivulets and cataracts, with a beautiful artificially-made pond in the centre.

Parks and Boulevards.

DEARBORN PARK.

The first, and for many years the only public park in the city, is an oblong piece of ground extending from Randolph to Washington street, and from Michigan avenue to Dearborn place, and contains one and a half acres. The ground was presented to the city by the United States, to be used for ever as a public Park. It is enclosed by a neat iron railing, and planted with trees.

JEFFERSON PARK

Is but two blocks south and one block east of Union Park, embracing but a single square, bounded by Monroe, Throop, Adams and Loomis streets. It contains about five acres. It is surrounded by stately and beautiful residences.

VERNON PARK

Is an oblong piece of ground about 300 feet wide by 600 feet long, on Centre avenue and West Polk street.

WOODLAND AND GROVELAND.

These are private parks laid out by the late Senator Douglas in the beautiful grove, in the South Division, called Oakenwald, and are intended for the especial benefit of the proprietors of the lots which front upon them.

WASHINGTON PARK

Is a small square between North Clark and Dearborn streets, north of Chesnut street, containing two and one half acres. It has a number of shade trees, and is quite a pleasant retreat from the dust and heat of a summer's day.

THE RIVER.

THE first recorded vessel that entered the harbor of Chicago, was the schooner Tracy, in 1803, under command of Lieut. Dorr, laden with supplies for the U. S. garrison in Fort Dearborn. Its condition at that time is not mentioned. Col. Long, of the engineers, who visited Chicago in 1816, found the river discharging itself into the lake over a bar of gravel and sand in a sluggish stream only a few inches deep, and from thirty to forty feet wide. In a broader, deeper, and much more copious stream the Little Calumet entered the lake over a similar bar about ten miles further south.

Seven years later, when Col. Long visited these places, he found the mouth of the Chicago River but little changed, while that of the Little Calumet was blocked up by a dry sand bar. The first steamboat that entered the Chicago river, was the Shelden Thompson, in 1832, during the Black Hawk war, bringing troops and provisions, with General Winfield Scott in command of the troops.

In 1833 Congress made the first appropriation of $30,000 to improve the harbor. The north pier was run out a short distance and a light-house erected. An embankment was made to cut off the river from her old channel, which had previously emptied into the lake near the foot of Madison street. This work was commenced in the summer of 1833, and vigorously pushed forward. In the following spring came a great freshet, which cleaned out the sand from the mouth, and did more work than all the dredges. In successive years additional appropriations were made, amounting in the aggregate to $144,000. In 1839 the work was suspended, the money having been exhausted. The constant current which sets toward the mouth of the river from the straits of Mackinaw, stirred up the sand and rolled it down into a huge bar in front of the city; the bar continued to accumulate, until, in 1864, it had reached the foot of Van Buren street, and vessels were compelled to tack round to that point, turn the bar, and beat up between it and the breakwater. Casualties, in consequence, became frequent. In order to prevent this continued accumulation of sand, the city at an early day began to extend the north pier out into the lake. It was first built out in a straight line 1,070 feet, then turning about 20 degrees to the north, 450 feet were added; thence on another plan 500 feet further, forming the arc of a circle; and reaching the site of the light-house erected in 1855, and which is situated 1,950 feet from the starting point. In 1864–5 450 feet more were added, continuing on the line of the first straight section. In 1866, Major J. D. Wheeler, of the Engineer Corps, in his report to the government, urged the erection of 600 feet additional to the north pier, and an appropriation of $88,704 was made for the purpose.

In 1816, when Col. Long examined the river, the stream was almost flush with the surrounding country. It was much narrower then than now. It was, however, much deeper, and is said to have had a depth of twenty feet near the present location of Clark street bridge; the widening of the stream and the heavy sediment constantly settling in its bed has sensibly diminished its depth.

In 1832 the two first bridges were built, one over the North Branch, at Water street, and another over the South Branch, between Lake and Randolph streets, the latter was not removed until 1840. It cost $486.20, which was raised by subscription, the Potawatomie Indians contributing nearly one-half the amount. The main channel is now crossed by substantial and costly swing-bridges at every second block in the more densely populated portions, and at frequent intervals beyond. Over the main channel are bridges at Rush, State, Clark and Wells streets, over the South Branch at Lake, Randolph, Madison, Van Buren, Polk, Twelfth, Eighteenth, Halsted, Reuben and Fuller streets, and at Archer Avenue. Over the North Branch at Kinzie, Indiana and Erie streets, Chicago Avenue, North Halsted street, North Avenue and Clybourne Avenue. The railroad trains cross the river on bridges built by the railroad companies. The public bridges require to be rebuilt about every five years. Their average cost is about $35,000.

When navigation first began upon this river, vessels were unable to go up the North Branch further than Chicago Avenue, and up the South Branch their progress was impeded at Eighteenth street. From this point to where the canal begins, a distance of one mile and a half, the river has been deepened and widened. The number of vessels moving on the river and its branches became so great that a widening of the stream was of necessity demanded. The dock limits had been laid out nearly following the original curvatures of the banks. It has been decided to widen the branches to an uniform width of two hundred feet, and the improvement is now being carried out, but it will take many years before it can possibly be completed. The established width for the main river is 250 feet, and in some points this is exceeded. The North Branch has been also deepened, and is now navigable one mile and a quarter beyond Chicago Avenue.

In 1848 the building of docks was fairly commenced. In 1854 the city had four miles of wharves. Now there are twelve miles in operation, having cost over $1,250,000. Four miles of this have been renewed, making a total of fifteen miles built. Dock piling lasts only about nine years. This dock system has extended immensely along the South Branch in the West Division. But a movement has recently commenced for the construction of a still greater system along the lake shore, just north of the mouth of the river.

North from the new pier previously mentioned, the Chicago Dock Company will build a breakwater 500 feet long; from the northern extremity of this a breakwater 1,500 feet in length will be constructed reaching to the shore. An area extending 390 feet north from the pier, and west to the shore of the lake, will be filled in, and through the center of this made land will run a street from the main shore to the eastern channel. The block thus created will be divided into lots for dockage purposes. On the north side of this made land there will be a channel, 110 feet wide, penetrating Michigan street as far as Sand street. The water in the basin will be twenty-two feet, and the largest vessels will easily float in the canal. The two will give as much wharfage as is now afforded by both sides of the river, as far as the confluence of the two branches.

This work was commenced in the beginning of 1867, and is being carried on in connection with the extension ordered by the Government — the work being really begun where the United States officials will cease their labors. This new line of pier will form a grand line of nearly 2,000 feet upon the North Side. The limited space at our disposal in a little work so circumscribed in its scope as a HAND-BOOK for strangers, prevents us from enlarging upon the subject of the Chicago River; we would refer the curious reader to the very best compend of Chicago, her history and statistics, that has ever appeared, and to which we are indebted for the above article (condensed) and much other valuable information,—we refer to "Historical and Statistical Sketch of Chicago," by E. Colbert.

THE LAKE TUNNEL.

SINCE the completion of this grand undertaking, the people of Chicago have enjoyed the inestimable blessing of an inexhaustible supply of the purest water in the world. For a long time previous to 1863, the water pumped up from the shore of the lake and supplied for drinking purposes was unfit for human use. After a long and careful consideration of various plans to remedy the crying evil, and secure a supply of pure water, the Board of Public Works decided early in 1863 to carry a tunnel out two miles under the bed of the lake.

On the 17th of March, 1864, ground was broken for the tunnel on the lot occupied by the Pumping works, at the east end of Chicago avenue, on the lake shore.

From the shore shaft, which is 67 feet deep, the tunnel extends two miles out in a straight line at right angles with the shore. The clear width of the tunnel is 5 feet, and the clear height 5 feet 2 inches, the top and bottom arches being semi-circles. It is lined with brick masonry 8 inches thick, in two wings or shells, the bricks being laid lengthwise of the tunnel, with toothing joints. The bottom of the inside surface of the bore at the east end is 66 feet below water level, with a gradual slope of two feet to the mile towards the shore shaft. This gives a clear fall of four feet in the whole distance, to permit the emptying of it in case of needed repairs, a gate at the crib shutting off the supply of water. The brick work has been laid in 8 inches thick all around, well set in cement.

The tunnel as now constructed will deliver under a head of two feet, 19,000,000 gallons of water daily; under a head of eight feet, 38,000,000 gallons daily, and under a head of eighteen feet, 57,000,000 gallons daily. The velocities for the above quantities will be one and four-tenths mile per hour, head being two feet; head being eight feet, the velocity will be two and three-tenths miles per hour, and the head being eighteen feet the velocity will be four and two-tenths miles per hour. By these means it will be competent to supply one million people with fifty-seven gallons each per day, with a head of eighteen feet.

The Crib, as it is called, in which is enclosed the east shaft of the tunnel, will repay a visit. It can be reached by the steam tugs from Clark street bridge. Excursions during the summer time are frequent.

The crib is forty feet and a half high, and built in pentagonal form, in a circumscribing circle of ninety-eight and a half feet in diameter. It is built of logs one foot square, and consists of three walls, at a distance of eleven feet from each other, leaving a central pentagonal space having an inscribed circle of twenty-five feet, within which is fixed the iron cylinder, nine feet in diameter, running from the water line to the tunnel, sixty-four feet below the surface and thirty-one feet below the bed of the lake at that point. The crib is thoroughly braced in every direction. It contains 750,000 feet of lumber, board measure, and 150 tons iron bolts. It is filled with 4,500 tons of stone and weighs 5,700 tons. The crib stands twelve feet above the water line, giving a maximum area of 1,200 feet which can be exposed at one sweep to the action of the waves, reckoning the resistance as perpendicular. The outside was thoroughly caulked, equal to a first-class vessel, with three threads in each seam, the first and last being what is called "horsed." Over all these there is a layer of lagging to keep the caulking in place and protect the crib proper from the action of the waves. A covered platform or house was built over the crib, enabling the workmen to prosecute the work uninterrupted by rain or wind, and affording a protection for the earth brought up from the excavation, and permitting it to be carried away by scows, whose return cargoes were bricks for the lining of the tunnel.

The first brick was laid at the crib end on the 22d of December, 1865, and on the last day of the year the workmen began to excavate from that end, at which time they had already 4,825 feet done from the shore. From that time the work progressed steadily and with few interruptions of any consequence. In the early part of November, 1866, when within a few feet of meeting, the workmen met for the first time with sand pockets, which caused leakage, and delayed the final blow till December 6th, when the last brick (which was a stone), was laid by Mayor J. B. Rice, in the presence of the Aldermen, city officials, and as many other prominent citizens as could be packed into the tunnel within hearing distance.

Still another delay was experienced in the construction of the conduits to the new pumping works, and it was not till Monday, March 25th, 1867, that the water was let into the tunnel to flow through the water pipes and hydrants of the city. On that day the new water works were formally inaugurated by the laying of the corner stone of a new tower, situated about half a block west of the old tower, and since completed to a total height of 130 feet, standing on a base of twenty-four feet square. Within this tower is an iron column three feet in internal diameter, to the top of which the water is forced from the tunnel by powerful pumping machinery, and is thence forced by its own pressure through the mains and to the tops of the highest buildings in the city. The column is surrounded by a neat spiral staircase. The machinery now employed to do this consists of three engines: No. 1, capable of pumping 18,000,000 gallons daily; engine No. 2, 12,000,000 gallons daily; and No. 3, 8,000,000 gallons daily, and the Board of Public Works have now asked the Council for authority to purchase a fourth engine, capable of pumping 36,000,000 gallons daily. This increase in the pumping facilities of these works is believed to be necessitated by the growth of the city; it being remembered that it is necessary to provide against accident to one of the engines, as the water supply ought not to be suspended during its repair.

COST.

The total cost of the lake tunnel to the city, including extras, preliminary examination, supervision, etc., is $457,845. The cost of the new water-tower, of the largest engine, and the building, now nearly finished for the reception of the machinery and the accommodation of the workmen, will swell the total to about $900,000. The total water debt of the city was £2,483,000 in April, 1867.

The total amount of water pipe laid in the city up to the close of 1868 was 228¼ miles.

The total capacity of pipes and reservoirs was 3,400,000 gallons.

There were about 900 fire hydrants and 450 stopcocks in the city at the beginning of the present year.

MORE WANTED.

With this tremendous increase, the city of Chicago is not supplied rapidly enough for its wants. The tunnel will admit the passage of water sufficient to supply one million of inhabitants, but the street pipes need extending and enlarging. Many of those nearest the water works were put down several years ago, and are now too small to feed those lying beyond. The difficulty is greatest in the West Division, and to obviate it a plan has been for some time under discussion to construct a tunnel starting from the present water works on the shore end of the tunnel, and running thence to a point in the West Division some where on the line of Union Park, with adequate pumping works, mains and distributing pipes diverging to every part of that division of the city.

THE RIVER TUNNELS.

ONE of the greatest curiosities to strangers visiting the city, is that gigantic undertaking in engineering science, the great pioneer sub-marine tunnel of the western hemisphere. The large number of vessels entering the port of Chicago, requiring the opening of bridges during the season of navigation every few minutes, greatly impeded the long lines of vehicles and pedestrians constantly passing over. The demand for a more eligible means of communication with the several divisions of the city became a necessity. A great public necessity in Chicago can never be long experiperienced; the people will have a remedy, regardless of cost.

On the 28th of October, 1864, the original ordinance for the construction of a tunnel under the Chicago river was passed by the city council. At this time the real magnitude of the undertaking was scarcely appreciated, and much valuable time was spent in discussing and considering the means and the location. It was at length determined to tax the entire city for the means, and Washington street was fixed on for the location and bids for the work advertised for.

On the 27th of July, 1866—nearly three years after the passage of the original ordinance—ground was broken on Washington street for the tunnel, by Messrs. Stewart, Ludlam & Co., to whom the contract had been awarded. They, however, were unfortunate in their mode of procedure, and finally abandoned the work in May, 1867. The contract was then taken by Messrs. J. K. Lake, C. B. Farwell, and A. A. McDonnell, the contract price being $328,500; and they, by a vigorous prosecution of the work, brought it to a successful completion on the first day of the new year 1869, when it was formally opened to the public in an appropriate, though unostentatious manner, the severity of the weather preventing any general public celebration. Subsequently the tunnel was subjected to a practical test of its capacity as a thoroughfare. Five teams were driven through the tunnel loaded heavily as follows: 6,445 lbs., 6,500 lbs., 7,280 lbs., 8,685 lbs., and 9,165 lbs. The weight of the wagons averaged 2,600 lbs. each. The horses were not selected with reference to their drawing capabilities, but were considered as average teams used for that purpose. Those drawing the heaviest load arrived at the top of the grade without showing any symptoms of having been overworked, and all of them went through with apparent ease. Experienced parties gave it as their opinion that loads of 5,000 and 6,000 pounds can be drawn through the tunnel, by ordinary horses, with ease, and with less effort than at many of the bridges. The Board of Public Works were well pleased with the experiment, and entirely satisfied that in this, as in all other respects, the tunnel is a complete success.

The tunnel is divided into two portions. That for vehicles dips from Franklin street on the east end, and Clinton street on the west end, forming an open passage way twenty-two feet wide in the middle of Washington street, for a distance of one block on each side of the river. For 332 feet from the entrance the tunnel comprises a single large chamber. It is 10 feet 6 inches at the entrance, and about 150 feet from the river center it increases to $23\frac{1}{2}$ feet. From the invert to the top of the arch the height is 20 feet 6 inches. The invert itself is 20 inches thick, being the segment of a circle 47.66 inches in diameter. At the base the abutments are 8 feet broad, until they reach the height of 5 feet 2 inches, when they continue 6 feet thick for 7 feet more. The arch is 32 feet thick at the sides, and 24 at top; is 9 feet above the springing lines, and has 3 centres. The spandrel backs are formed of rubble masonry. The chamber at 150 feet distance from the river centre is 18 feet high, the inverts 16 inches thick, the abutments 7 feet 2 inches at base for a height of 3 feet 4 inches, then 6 feet thick for another foot, and 5 feet thick at top. The height above the springing arch is 7¾ feet here. This section extends 364 feet on the west side, and has a corresponding section on the east side, which extends 269 feet. At 110 feet from the river centre, on either side, separate double wagon-ways begin. Each are 11 feet wide and 15 high. A thick wall divides them, and supports and strengthens the work directly beneath the river bed. The two ends of the passage correspond. Parallel with the carriage-way the foot-passage extends 11 feet high at the centre, and 6 at the sides of the arch. A flooring of white pine is laid on joists, making a good even surface. The lights are 40 feet apart here and 50 in the carriage-way. Entrances are pierced through the walls to the roadways and the other footway.

Neat passenger houses, of Tuscan style, each 22 feet long by 19 feet 4 inches wide, stand on either side of the river over the passenger entrance. Eighteen steps are in each house. Ventilation shafts are sunk 110 feet from the entrance, and by these and other arrangements the air of the tunnel will be kept fresh.

The following is a table of the dimensions and grades of the tunnel:

From centre of Franklin to center of Clinton street, 1,603 feet.

Between arches, 930 feet.

Between entrances to passage way, 810 feet.

Grade of descent westward from Franklin street, 1 in 16, for distance of 306 feet.

Grade of descent eastward from Clinton street, 1 in 18, for distance of 625 feet.

Depth of river channel, at tunnel, 16 feet.

Between walls, at Franklin and Clinton streets, 23½ feet; at arches, 19½ feet.

Height of river section, 18.83 feet; of approaches, 20½ feet.

Total length of Nicholson pavement, laid on Joliet gravel, 1,608 feet.

The visitor will better understand the magnitude of the enterprise by the following statistics:

From July, 1868, to December 31st, 1869, 600,000

hours of mechanics and laborer's work have been expended in its construction; 45,000 cubic yards of clay excavated; 5,000 cubic yards of cement laid; 6,000 of brick, and 10,000 of stone masonry; 10,000 of broken stone and sand, and 20,000 barrels of Falls City cement. In addition to the manual labor, a large amount of horse and steam labor was used, and several stone quarries were engaged in getting out the stone for the abutments and arches, not to mention the manufacture of the brick, which of itself gave employment to a large number of workmen.

A few items of comparison with the celebrated Thames Tunnel in London, England, will be found interesting to the visitor. The Thames Tunnel was built for the purpose of effecting a ready communication for wagons and pedestrians between the Middlesex and Surrey sides of the river, at a point below London bridge, where it is inconvenient to erect a bridge on account of the width of the river and the heavy East Indiamen and other vessels passing up to the docks. The approaches have never been graded. Over each of these shafts a small house is erected, and the descent is by a winding staircase. Devised by Sir Isambart Brunel, it was commenced in the year 1825, but was not opened until 1843, and has never yet been finished, and probably never will be. It consists of two arched avenues, 1,200 feet long, lighted by gas, and cost £500,000 sterling, or $2,500,000 in gold. Its income has never paid its incidental expenses. In every foot are 6,000 bricks, and its external dimensions are 37 feet 6 inches in width, and 22 feet in height. During its construction the river broke through five times, great loss of life resulting from the irruption of the water.

It seems Fate decreed that the construction of a *successful* tunnel should be deferred for the young city of the Western World!

MORE TUNNELS.

The experiment of a tunnel under the river having proved to be a success in the case of the Washington street tunnel, it is now proposed to construct one at Adams street and another one at LaSalle street. From a communication addressed to the City Council by Mr. E. S. Chesborough, the distinguished city engineer, we gather the following interesting items :

The plan proposed for LaSalle street is in the main features very similar to the one already constructed at Washington street. Its total length, including approaches from Randolph street on the south and Michigan street on the north will be 1,930 feet. The net estimate for the work is $457,342.32, but in view of the possibility of occurrences difficult now to foresee, an appropriation of $500,000 is asked for.

The plan proposed for the Adams street tunnel is very much the same. The total length, extending from the west side of Franklin to the east side of Clinton street, is 1,527 feet, and the estimated cost about $400,000. It is proposed that the work shall be prosecuted night and day, and during the winter that the river portion shall be roofed over to preserve in it at all times a temperature above freezing, so that no interruption shall occur from the inclemency of the weather.

THE ARTESIAN WELLS,

SITUATED on the corner of Chicago and Western avenues, will well repay the trouble of a visit. They are readily accessible by the Randolph street horse cars to the city limits, where a few minutes' walk will enable the visitor to reach the ground where they are situated. The tract of land was bought by a company in 1863, during the oil fever, for the purpose of boring for oil, under the inspiration of a spiritual medium, who asserted the existence of large quantities oil underlying the tract; also, that beneath this ground there was a "well of the purest, best and healthiest water known any where, which would reach to the surface with great force and power, and in quantities to supply the people of this city for all time to come." The boring commenced in December, 1863, with a diameter of five inches, but had to be abandoned in the following

January, in consequence of the tools getting fast in the bottom of the well. In February, 1864, another boring was commenced, and proceeded slowly until November of the same year, when, at a depth of 711 feet below the surface, water was struck, and has continued to flow steadily and constantly at the rate of 600,000 gallons daily. In May, 1865, a twenty feet overshot wheel, with the necessary machinery for boring, was constructed, and a second well commenced, the power being furnished by the water from the first well, which was carried up 25 feet above the surface in a 3½ inch flume, whence it discharged over the wheel. This second well is located about nine feet from the first. On the 1st of November following, at a depth of 694 feet 4 inches, water was reached. The boring continued to a depth of 1,100 feet. It is estimated that the two wells are now flowing about one and a quarter million gallons every twenty-four hours. During the progress of the boring, about one hundred gallons of petroleum was secured by pumping. There are two other Artesian wells in the Union Stock Yards, which are described on another page.

THE UNION STOCK YARDS.

No visitor to Chicago should fail in seeing this, the great bovine city of the world, the live-stock market of the north-west. The advantages offered by this mammoth enterprise to western dealers and feeders are unequalled in any market either in the old or new world. The enterprise is owned by a chartered company with a paid-up capital of one million dollars. The grounds consist of 345 acres of land extending from Halsted street on the east to the south branch of the river, and from Egan Avenue on the north, thence south on the open prairie. The yards connect by special tracks with all railroads centering in Chicago, hence, stock can be received or shipped by or to any line, at all times with the readiest dispatch. The connecting lines with the Stock Yards, were constructed by the Union Stock

Yard and Transportation Companies, and are about twenty-one miles in length. The entire 345 acres of land comprised in the Union Stock Yards are laid out in streets and alleys in the same manner as a large city. Through the centre, from north to south, runs a broad avenue called Avenue E. It is one mile in length, and seventy-five feet in breadth, and divided into three sections, like a bridge, to facilitate the driving of cattle through it. Droves passing to the south take one section, those to the north another, passing on the way without any inconvenience or stoppage. This avenue intersects the entire grounds, and is paved with Nicholson pavement. There is not in Chicago a finer or a smoother drive than it. It presents a very animated scene when the yards are filled with countless herds of cattle and swine, and teeming with the bustle and activity of buying, selling and transporting stock. Running parallel to Avenue E, are other streets, leading to the railroads that surround the yards, and to different sections. These streets are crossed at right angles by others running east and west — the principal of which passes by the Stock Yards hotel, and has been aptly named "Broadway." It leads from the hotel to the Bank and Exchange Building, where the life and excitement of the yards centre. It is sixty six feet wide, planked with heavy plank, and traversed on the side by a raised sidewalk. It is so curved as to carry off the water into drains, somewhat similar to the roof of a building. Parallel to Broadway run other streets and avenues, which cross Avenue E at right angles, dividing the whole into blocks like a well-laid-out city. The irregular streets are caused by the curves made for the railroads, but they lead off directly into the regular avenues. These are all designated by letters and numbers, as are all the pens and different stalls and yards. The pens for cattle and sheep vary in size, but are nearly all laid out in rectangular shape. They are so constructed that several can be thrown into one by merely opening gates, like the rooms of a house. Gates are also so arranged as to open across the road, turning a drove directly into the pen, and closing after them. In size, these enclosures vary from 20x25 feet, to

85x112 feet, while others are precisely the size of a car, calculated to hold just a car-load of stock. These latter are mostly arranged near the shoots at the different railroads. The posts supporting the fences which form these pens are cedar, sunk through holes in the planking and three feet into the ground. They average about six feet apart all over the grounds. The cattle pens are open, but those designed for hogs are covered with sheds. The yards are provided with ample hay-barns and corn-cribs, situated in different parts of the enclosure, convenient to different sections of pens. These barns are 30x150 feet long, one story high, and are capable of holding 500 tons of hay each. The corn-cribs are each near one of the barns. Their average capacity is six thousand bushels of corn. The arrangements for loading and unloading are as nearly perfect as it is possible to conceive. Each railroad has one thousand feet of unloading track for its own use exclusively, and a corresponding array of shoots which are so arranged that whole trains can be unloaded at once. The arrangements are so perfect that any number of cattle can easily be transferred from one road to another without any risk of loss.

It is now proposed to cut a canal 160 feet wide from the south branch of the river along Egan Avenue to the cattle yards, of sufficient capacity to float vessels. The river is already navigable to within a short distance of where the canal will enter it, and the remainder can be easily dredged out. Vessels can then come directly in front of the yards, and depart thence to any port. This will afford greater facilities to the packing-houses which will be built in that region, as their products can be shipped without the expense of handling consequent upon shipping from our present docks.

The company have now about 180 acres of land reserved for future contingencies.

The following table gives the size, number of pens, etc., belonging to this market:

	ACRES.
Quantity of land owned by the U. S. Y. and Transit Company	845
Number of Acres in Pens	120
Number of Acres used for Hotel and other buildings	47
Number of Acres reserved for new Pens	178

The Union Stock Yards.

STOCK CAPACITY.—The Yards will conveniently contain, at one and the same time, the following numbers of Stock:

	HEAD.
Cattle	25,000
Hogs	100,000
Sheep	50,000
Stalls for Horses	850
Total capacity	175,850

There are, for the thorough drainage of the Yards, 35 miles of under drains. The streets and alleys occupy 10 miles of length. There are 2,000 open Stock Pens, or yards for Cattle; 1,000 covered pens for Hogs and Sheep, and 2,700 gates. The pens, whether covered or open, are all of them well fitted with troughs and hydrants, the latter connected with the water tanks. For the information of the curious we may state, that the corn troughs, if placed close together, would occupy a line five miles in length, and the feed troughs, if used after the same fashion, would make a line 15 miles in length.

Since the opening of the second Artesian Well, an unlimited and indeed inexhaustible supply of pure water is obtained for watering stock and all other useful purposes. The following particulars respecting these valuable wells will be read with interest:

THE FIRST STOCK YARD WELL.

A well 8 feet in depth was dug, in which, on the 14th of May, 1866, drilling was commenced. Six feet of downward progress were made the first day, 3 the second, 9 the third, 2 the fourth, 8 the eighth, and 4 the ninth.

The greatest progress was made on the 29th of October, when 64 feet were drilled. On the 20th of the same month 46 feet were made; 36 feet on the 13th, and 36 feet on the 6th. With these exceptions, and 34 feet drilled on the 1st of June and 20 on the 2nd, the daily amount of drilling was of a much smaller extent, and probably did not average more than 8 or 10 feet. Several minor streams of water were encountered, but it was not until the 30th of October that the final stream was reached. On this day 22 feet were drilled, making a total depth of 1,032 feet. From this well 65,000 gallons of water were yielded daily, and for a time it was supposed that, with this great increase of the company's water-power, it would be fully able to satisfy the requirements of the yards; but the lapse of a very few months showed the necessity of at least a second visitation to the depths below.

THE LAST STOCK YARD WELL.

Determined to get enough of the required fluid, the management, in the spring of 1867, instituted the preliminary arrangements for sinking a second well. Boring was commenced on or about the 14th of May, 1868, and on the 24th of February, after passing two steeams of water, a vein was struck at the depth of 1,190 feet, which at the surface yields the unprecedented quantity of 600,000 gallons a day.

These two wells, perfectly dissimilar in many of their essential characteristics, wonderfully different in the quantity of water yielded, yet only separated one from the other by the distance of a few lineal feet, have attracted considerable attention since their completion. They have been visited by large numbers of scientific and practical men, and are justly regarded as works of no mean importance in the scientific world.

THE TWO WELLS

are both beneath the same shed, and fill three tanks that rest side by side. Each tank is elevated 45 feet from the ground, and has a capacity of holding 114,000 gallons. The wells are 59 feet apart north and south, in which distance the strata has a "dip" or inclination of seven feet to the north-east. In the old well the first bed of sandstone is 20 feet thicker than in the new one. The stratum of underlying limestone is exactly twenty feet thinner. With this exception, both borings present materially the same features.

THE WATER

in the wells presents a marked and singular difference. In the old well it is strongly impregnated with sulphur.

So thoroughly is the impregnation, that the water not only smells and tastes of the substance, but deposits it profusely upon the bottom of the trough in which it is received, and in the tank in which it is collected. After exposure to the air for a few hours, the sulphur is partly precipitated and partly carried off by the air, leaving a perfectly colorless and tasteless fluid.

In the second well, on the other hand, there are no sulphurous evidences; but the water is strongly charged with one of the oxides of iron. It has no perceptible odor, but its chalybeate characteristics are very apparent to the taste, and to the eye in the iron-brown deposit which covers the bottom of the receiving trough. Both waters undoubtedly possess excellent medical properties, and, if only situated in some fashionable watering place, would undoubtedly boast a national reputation.

THE FORCE OF THE WATER

of the last well is sufficient to discharge 600,000 gallons a day at the surface. In carrying itself to the height of the tanks, an altitude of forty-five feet from the ground, it loses so much force that only 450,000 gallons are discharged at this point daily. It is estimated that at a further height of 130 feet, being 175 from the surface, the water would assume a stationary position.

The wells are both now in running operation at the stock-yards. They are the only means used in the supply of the immense amount of water there constantly required, and prove highly successful in every respect. As living realizations of the laws of science; as proud exemplifications of the energy and will of our people, they should command the interest and attention of every believer in Chicago and her institutions.

THE UNION STOCK-YARD EXCHANGE AND BANK.

The Union Stock-Yard National Bank, whose offices are at the yards, is one of the most effective auxiliaries in facilitating the general business of the market we have. It was not founded as a mere commercial enterprise, for in the outset its promoters must have seen divers ways of investing their capital of a more promising and remunerative character; but such an institution was an absolute necessity, and had therefore to be provided. When the live-stock markets of Chicago, for we had several, were located at a comparatively short distance from the Court-house, access to city banks was easy, but by removing the market away out on the prairie, and beyond the city limits, due provision was needful for the security and transmission of such large sums of money as are handled in this special business. The undertaking has proved a great success, and is receiving the support of all prominent live-stock operators in the West. This structure is built of brick, and is two stories high, surmounted by four gables, which give it a novel and picturesque appearance. It stands on the corner of avenues D and E. The south end of the building constitutes the bank. The room is thirty-seven feet square, and provided with an immense stone vault, said to be the strongest in the city, and capable of withstanding the chisels and powder of any number of burglars. Adjoining the bank is the office of the Secretary of the company, a room 20 by 37 feet, with a door opening into a separate compartment of the vault. The remainder of the ground floor is a large room 60 by 80 feet, known as the Exchange. On the second floor are twelve commodious rooms, two of which, in the east end, are used as telegraph offices, and the others rented to brokers and others doing business at the yards.

HOTEL.

For the accommodation of drovers and business men, as well as visitors to the yards, a capacious hotel has been erected, called the "Hough House." The edifice cost $125,000. It is 30 feet front by 144 feet deep, and six stories high. It fronts on Halsted street, and stands on the south-east corner of the yards proper. It is built of light-colored brick, with a Mansard roof, and surmounted with a cupola with a globe-like top and a weather-vane. On the front of the hotel extends a verandah fifty-two feet in length, which is reached by a flight of about twenty broad steps, running the entire length, the whole bordered by a handsome railing similar to that which borders the balcony of the cupola. On the south side, which looks out upon the prairie, is a similar verandah, eighty-four feet in length, entered by the windows and several doors which open upon it. From this point a most delightful view is afforded. On a warm summer day this is one of our most enjoyable suburban retreats.

THE SLOPE OF THE PACIFIC AND THE NEW WEST.

THOUGH we have hewn out a way through the desert, and found enough to convince us that the best part of the continent remains unsettled, our knowledge of the vast region lying west of the Missouri is very slight, and exceedingly superficial, and no wonder, when we consider that up to the year 1844, just a quarter of a century ago, there were no white men more than a giant's stone-throw west of the "Big Muddy." Within that twenty-five years, since Polk sat in the White House, and Louis Napoleon played his grand *coup d'etat*, we have gathered all we know of a region equal in extent to the whole of European Russia, which has a population of seventy million souls. No wonder that the surveyor's chain has been dragged over but infinitesimal portions of the vast area, and that section lines are few, though claims innumerable have been staked off, and millions of dollars worth of the precious metals dragged from the volcanic repose of centuries by the adventurous searcher after gold.

The following statistics will give a clearer idea of the extent of the country yet to be conquered, and help us to a better comprehension of what they may become in the future, than a volume of mere verbal description:

TERRITORY AND POPULATION.

The following shows the area in square miles of the several States and Territories within the district of the New West, with the population in 1860, and estimated population at the present time:

	Sq. Miles.	Pop. 1860.	Pop. 1869.
Alaska	577,890	Not in	75,000
Arizona	113,916	Org. '63	25,000
California	188,991	379,994	580,000
Colorado	104,500	34,277	55,000
Dakota	152,000	4,837	80,000
Idaho	90,932	Org. '68	45,000
Indian Territory	68,991	9,761	10,000
Kansas	81,318	107,206	300,000
Montana	143,776	Org. '64	60,000
Nebraska	75,995	28,826	80,000
Nevada	112,000	6,857	53,000
New Mexico	121,201	93,516	......
Oregon	95,274	52,455	100,000
Utah	88,056	40,244	130,000
Washington Territory	69,994	11,594	10,000
Wyoming	88,000	Org. '68	5,000
Total	2,172,416	769,577	1,579,000
Total of U. S. and Ter.	3,578,392	27,489,561	41,000,000
Per cent	60.7	2.8	3.85

Including Alaska (70,000) this area contains about 210,000 Indians.

More than sixty per cent. of the whole territory of the United States lies west of the Missouri proper, without reference to that part which lies west of the Mississippi below the confluence of the two mighty rivers. The whole of this territory is virtually opened up to us of the "East" by the Pacific Railroad, and will, ere long, be actually opened up by its branches. Thus more than 2,000,000 square miles contained but 2.8 per cent., or 10 in 357 of the entire population of the United States and territories in 1860. At present it contains one twenty-sixth part of the entire population, the number being about double what it was nine years ago. These figures will not necessarily show what will be the growth of the next nine years, but they do show how much of room and opportunity exists for it, and no one can doubt that, with the opportunities and facilities afforded by the Pacific Railroad, their future growth will be so great that the increase of the past will be too short a rod to measure it by.

PROPERTY VALUATIONS.

The following were the property valuations, real and personal, of these States and Territories in 1850 and 1860, as then bounded:

The New West.

	1850.	1860.
California	$22,161,872	$207,874,613
Kansas		31,327,895
Oregon	5,063,474	28,930,637
Nebraska		9,131,056
New Mexico	5,174,471	20,818,768
Utah	986,083	5,526,118
Washington Territory		5,691,466
Totals	$ 33,385,900	$329,275,543
Totals U. S.	7,135,780,228	$16,159,616,068
Per cent to whole	0.42	1.85

A valuation on the same scale to-day would give not less than $25,000,000,000, of which about 1,000,000,000, or four per cent., belongs to the New West, as against one part in 217 in 1850, and one part in 54 in 1860.

MANUFACTURES.

The following shows the principal manufacturing statistics for 1860:

	Capital.	Hands Employed.	Value of Product.
California	$22,043,096	49,221	$68,253,228
Kansas	1,084,935	1,785	4,357,408
Nebraska	266,575	336	607,328
Oregon	1,337,238	978	2,976,761
Utah	443,856	889	900,153
Washington Territory	1,296,200	870	1,406,921
Totals	$26,471,400	53,529	$78,502,799
Total U. S. & T.	1,009,855,715	1,811,246	1,885,861,676
Per cent	2.6	4	4.16

It is significant of the energies of a *new* country, that 4 per cent. of the workers in the United States occupied the New West in 1860, while it contained less than 3 per cent. of the population. There were few or no idlers, and are few now—a fact which speaks volumes for its future. The number of workers has about doubled within the past nine years, and it is safe to assume that the capital actually employed has more than trebled within the same period, irrespective of the increased value of land.

BANKS.

The following shows the number, capital, and circulation, in September, 1868, of the National Banks west

of the Missouri, except for California, which has no
National Banks. That State has a total of thirty-four
private bankers, and the State Bank has a capital of
$5,000,000.

	No.	Capital.	Circulation.
Kansas	5	$490,000	$351,000
Nebraska	4	850,000	170,000
Colorado	3	850,000	254,500
Nevada	1	155,000	131,700
Oregon	1	100,000	89,500
Utah	1	150,000	135,500
Montana	1	100,000	86,000
Idaho	1	100,000	63,000
Totals	17	$1,705,000	$1,283,700
Total for United States	1,629	426,189,111	809,915,166
Per cent	1	0.4	0.4

The following was the estimated yield of the precious
metals in 1868:

California	$20,000,000
Nevada	18,000,000
Montana	12,000,000
Idaho	6,000,000
Oregon	5,000,000
Colorado	4,000,000
Washington	1,000,000
Arizona	250,000
New Mexico	250,000
Total	$66,500,000

The annual yield is equal to about $20\frac{1}{2}$ per cent. of
the entire banking circulation of the Union, or sufficient
to redeem it all in the course of less than five years,
even in its present ratio. Estimating the total value
as equal only to ten years' product, it gives a specie
basis of $540 for every dollar of paper confided to the
care of the people of the New West. But this yield
will be largely increased as the facilities for transporting men and machinery are opened up by the Pacific
Railroad. It is safe to estimate that the above tabu-
lated annual yield of gold and silver will be doubled
within the next four years.

Nebraska increased her corn area last year by 16,145
acres, or about twenty-five per cent. Kansas showed a
similar increase of 63,411 acres, or thirty per cent.;

while Iowa added to her corn area 236,682 acres, or fifteen per cent.

VOTES.

The States and Territories west of the Missouri gave last year a total of 173,202 votes, as follows: Kansas, 11,698; Idaho, 5,320; California, 108,670; Oregon, 22,086; Arizona, 2,093; Nebraska, 15,168; Colorado, 8,167. This was but about one vote to every 11½ squares miles of territory.

PRODUCTIONS.

The following are a few of the leading statistics of the productive and commercial industries of California in 1868:

Cocoons of silk (from 1,175,000 trees)	1,850,000
Eggs silk worms, do	1,850
Vintage, gallons	8,500,000
Vintage brandy, gallons	800,000
Vessels built	57
Tonnage	7,604
Passengers to and from Asia	10,095
Freights to and from Asia, tons	18,295
Deposits in (9) savings banks	$23,000,000
Increase by emigration, persons	85,000
Boots and shoes imported, packages	68,709
Domestic lumber, feet	197,672,000
Candles imported, boxes	264,589
Cigars imported, cases	445
Coal imported, anthracite, tons	29,592
English coal imported, tons	29,561
Australian coal imported, tons	27,000
Pig iron imported, tons	16,659
Iron, bars	814,683
Flour exported, brls	461,868
Wheat exported, bu	4,099,115

VALUE OF MERCHANDISE EXPORTS.

To New York	$8,541,976
To Great Britain	4,568,747
To Mexico	1,708,451
To South America	580,822
To Hawaiian Islands	803,746
To China	1,161,020
To British Columbia	918,589
To Japan	491,105
To Australia	1,035,835
To other countries	1,198,100
Total 1868	$22,948,840
Total 1867	22,465,908
Total 1866	17,808,018

	Total. Treas. a..d Mdse.
Treasure Exports, 1868.................$35,444,895	$58,887,775
" " 1867....................41,676,792	64,142,695
" " 1866....................44,864,894	61,667,411
Receipts of customs...........................	8,557,081
Receipts of customs, 1767....................	7,611,958
Coinage 1868.................................	17,865,000
Vessels, arrived, 8,259; tonnage..............	1,085,016
Sales for fiscal year 1867-8..................	$10,529,930
Commercial brokers' do......................	6,889,800
Wholesale dealers............................	188,438,290
Miscellaneous................................	47,367,264
Total sales of the year.......................	$253,218,884

The statistics of vessels building are believed to include the whole Pacific coast.

That the growth of California and Oregon will be wonderfully stimulated by the "great event" there can be no question. California expects to more than double her exports of breadstuffs this year, and her commerce will increase in much the same proportion by the opening up of a direct avenue of trade between China and Japan through the ports of San Francisco and Sacramento, while her population will, probably, show a duplication of the augment of 1868. Yet the future of California is not more brilliant than that of the interior States; they will, probably, grow even more rapidly than she has done, for their wealth is but just being discovered, and we are only just beginning to be able to reach them.

The value of direct shipments of the precious metals from Colorado in 1868, not including that taken by private hands, was......................................	$2,107,285
Of which gold amounted to...........................	1,909,461
And silver to.......................................	197,744
Value of agricultural products, 1868................	2,683,840

	Cultivation, acres.	Av. bu.
Wheat...............................	7,410	28
Corn................................	10,834	25
Oats, barley, etc....................	8,709	85
Potatoes.............................	1,966	100
Total acres.........................	23,919	

The railroad now building to connect the Pacific trunk line with the far-famed Pike's Peak region, opening up the Colorado parks and exposing its mineral treasures to the labor of the miner, as to the light of day, will make the preceding figures small by comparison with those of 1870.

MISCELLANEOUS.

The following are statistics of the Territory of Wyoming for 1868:

Letters mailed, No	505,696
Letters received, No	536,243
Stamps cancelled	$16,143
Stamps and stamped envelopes sold	$12,409
Gross sales merchandise	7,300,000
Paid for freight, exclusive of government	2,163,855
Value lumber sold	825,000
Receipts, passenger and express (W., F. & Co.)	804,000
Average cash deposited in banks	680,000
Loans and discounts	180,000
Eastern exchange sold	16,200,000
Cash paid over bank counters	25,400,000
Gold bought by banks	110,000
Freight received, lbs	74,010,654

And this is the youngest born into the sub-family of the Territories. Cheyenne alone promises to beat this exhibit next year.

The following are some of the productive statistics of Utah Territory for the year 1868:

Acres under cultivation	130,000
Of which the cereals comprise	80,000
Sugar cane	2,000
Root crops	6,800
Cotton	200
Apples	900
Peaches	1,000
Grapes	75
Currants	195
Meadow	80,000
Acres irrigated in 1867	94,000
Cost of same	$247,002
Property value in 1868	$10,533,879
Tax assessed on do	$52,666
Schools (in 186 districts, 13,000 pupils)	228
Property valuation of Salt Lake country	$4,879,650

This is what the Mormons have done—created it out of dead sterility. They have helped to build the Pacific Railroad, and are even now building a railroad for themselves, to make direct connection with the heart of Utah and the world's highway. It is more than probable that Utah will grow, too.

DISTANCES.

The following table shows the distances of the principal points on the route of the Pacific Railroad, each way, with the elevation in feet above the sea level:

	Distance, miles.	Elevation.	Distance, miles.
New York................	....	....	3,350
Chicago.................	960	625	2,890
Omaha..................	463	957	1,897
Kearney................	683	2,128	1,707
North Platte............	784	2,830	1,606
Cheyenne...............	1,009	6,062	1,881
Sherman (Summit)......	1,042	8,262	1,848
Bryan...................	1,854	6,810	1,036
Wahsatch...............	1,462	6,880	928
Weber Canon............	1,517	4,654	873
Ogden (Salt Lake).......	1,528	4,390	862
Promontory Point........	1,581	4,948	809
Humboldt Wells.........	1,750	5,650	640
Elcho (White Pine)......	1,810	5,630	580
Summit Sierra...........	2,165	7,042	225
Colfax..................	2,216	2,448	174
Sacramento.............	2,270	56	120
San Francisco...........	2,390	....	....

The following shows the distances in miles, and the time consumed in traveling, between Chicago and San Francisco:

	Miles.	Hours.
Chicago to Omaha.......................	493	24¼
Omaha to Cheyenne.....................	516	25¼
Cheyenne to Ogden (Utah)..............	519	28
Ogden to Elcho.........................	282	12¼
Elcho to Sacramento....................	460	16
Sacramento to San Francisco............	120	13¼
Totals........................	2,390	220

The rates of fare west of Ogden City are 10 cents per mile in gold, but it is expected that they will be materially reduced after the 1st of July. (For the above deeply interesting article, we are indebted to the Chicago *Tribune* of May 10th, 1869.)

UNIVERSITIES AND COLLEGES.

UNIVERSITY OF CHICAGO.

Is located within four miles of the Court House, and on the route of the Cottage Grove horse-cars, within a few steps of the shore of Lake Michigan. It is conducted under the auspices of the Baptist denomination, but is founded on a broad and liberal basis. It is built on a beautiful tract of ground donated by Hon. S. A. Douglas. It was founded in 1855, and the first building erected in 1858. The main central building is 126x172 feet, and was completed in 1868, at a cost of $110,000. It is of Athens marble, and is of very imposing appearance. The property, with endowments, is valued at $400,000.

OBSERVATORY.

With the extension of the Chicago University, it was determined to found an observatory which should be an honor to the west. A number of scientific gentlemen met and pledged their assistance. It was at first proposed to procure a small instrument from New York, but it was soon decided that Chicago wanted no makeshift, and the celebrated Clark telescope was secured, which had been made to the order of a Louisiana college, but not taken owing to the breaking out of the war. An observatory costing $30,000 was built on the western side of the University, and in 1864 the telescope was brought here and put in position, Prof. T. H. Safford being appointed Astronomer. The tower is called "the Dearborn." It is a massive octagonal structure, comprising a solid, isolated stone pier (the cap or tripod stone of which weighs over seven tons) within an octagonal stone tower 35 feet on the base, the whole surmounted by a revolving dome, which covers the room except in one point, where the telescope is pointed through an aperture. The following are the dimensions of the great Equatorial telescope, which moves by clock-work, keeping pace with the

UNIVERSITY OF CHICAGO.

Universities and Colleges.

revolutions of the earth on her axis, so that when once pointed to a star it will keep pace with it in its ethereal journey as long as may be needed to complete the required observation:
Diameter of Declination Circle, 30 inches.
Diameter of Hour Circle, 22 inches.
Focal Length of Object Glass, 23 feet.
Aperture of Object Glass, 18½ inches.

The circles are read by two microscopes each, the hour circle to seconds of time, and the declination circle to ten seconds of space. The Observatory has also a chronometer, and a small astronomical library.

A meridian circle of the first class has been constructed by Messrs. A. Repsold & Sons, of Hamburgh. This instrument has a telescope of six French inches aperture, and divided circles of forty inches diameter; otherwise it is like Bessel's celebrated Kœnigsberg circle, by the same makers, with some late improvements in the illumination of the field and the wires, and with apparatus for recording declinations, a new invention of the makers.

THE PRESBYTERIAN THEOLOGICAL SEMINARY

Is situated on the corner of Fullerton avenue and North Halsted street. The building was erected in 1863. This Seminary was founded in 1859 by the Old School General Assembly of the Presbyterian Church. The edifice is a very handsome building of pressed brick, 72 by 40 feet, with stone facings and caps, the basement being also of stone. The entire height is five stories. The Seminary has two libraries of nearly 7,000 volumes. The property is valued at $200,000.

THE CHICAGO THEOLOGICAL SEMINARY,

Located on Warren street, corner of Reuben street, was chartered in 1855. It belongs to the Congregational Church, but is open to the students of all denominations. Tuition is gratuitous to all students, and those who need it receive aid to the amount of $150 per year. The building is in the Norman style of architecture, a monument to the enterprise and liberality of the denomination. It has a frontage on Union Park of 155 feet, and another on Warren street of 120 feet.

THE NORTHWESTERN METHODIST EPISCOPAL UNIVERSITY

Is now located at Evanston, twelve miles north of the city. It was founded in Chicago in 1852. The buildings are magnificent. The total value of the property is about $600,000. There are now nearly two hundred students in the institution.

THE GARRETT BIBLICAL INSTITUTE,

A Methodist institution, is also located at Evanston. It was founded in 1855, and has now over one hundred students. The property is worth about $400,000.

UNIVERSITY OF ST. MARY'S OF THE LAKE,

Is situated on Superior street, near North State street. It was established in 1844, and a fine new building erected in 1863, under the presidency of the Rev. Dr. McMullen. It is now used only for the Seminarians, or candidates for priestly orders in the Catholic Church for the Diocese of Chicago.

COLLEGE OF ST. IGNATIUS.

This is a new college now in course of erection on West Twelfth street, corner of Blue Island Avenue, and adjoining the Church of the Holy Family. The building, when completed, will be one of the handsomest educational structures in the country. It is built of light colored pressed brick, with stone trimmings, and will cost $250,000. It will be under the charge of the Jesuit Fathers, and will accommodate a very large number of students. It is expected that it will be ready for the reception of students by the opening of the coming year.

Universities and Colleges. 75

CHRISTIAN BROTHERS ACADEMY.

ACADEMY OF THE CHRISTIAN BROTHERS.

The Academy of the Christian Brothers, on Van Buren street, near Clark, was first opened in the spring of 1868, and has already achieved a very high and deserved celebrity. In the Order of the Christian Brothers, founded for the purpose of devoting themselves to the education of youth, the members are trained especially to fulfill the duties of teachers. How well they perform the onerous duties of their calling, is attested by the great success and popularity of their schools in Europe, and of late years in this country. Students of all denominations are received, and the religious opinions of the parents respected and never interfered with in the child. The Academy at 99 Van Buren street is a large and well-appointed building, erected for the purpose at a cost of $60,000, under the directorship of Bro. Francis de Sales, one of the most accomplished and successful teachers this celebrated order has amongst them.

LAW SCHOOL.

Connected with the University of Chicago, but nearly independent in its operation, is a Law School, conducted in Oriental building, LaSalle street. Henry Booth, Esq., is Dean.

MEDICAL COLLEGES.

RUSH MEDICAL COLLEGE,

Located on the corner of Indiana and North Dearborn street, was established in 1843. The new building, erected in 1857 at a cost of $70,000, is one of the finest educational structures in the West. The College possesses a large and well-selected library, besides ample chemical apparatus, a laboratory, and a museum filled with every needed means of illustration and study in all the varied branches of medical science.

Universities and Colleges.

RUSH MEDICAL COLLEGE.

THE CHICAGO MEDICAL COLLEGE.

This institution, formerly the medical department of Lind University, was established in 1858, and is now in a prosperous condition. The spacious building it occupies, on the corner of State and Twenty-second streets, was erected in 1864, and, with the lot, cost $20,000.

THE HAHNEMANN MEDICAL COLLEGE,

Located at number 619 State street, was established in 1855 at 161 Clark street, and removed to its present location, in a fine new building, in February, 1868. As its name indicates, it is devoted to the preparation of practitioners of the Homœopathic system of medicine.

SCHOOLS.

The education of the youth of Chicago has, from the very earliest period in the history of the City, engaged the earnest and most solicitous attention of her citizens, and to-day the public, private, and secular schools of Chicago will bear favorable comparison with any city on the continent. The rapid growth of the city has rendered it a continuous difficulty to keep pace in accommodation for the scholars claiming admission. The present system of public schools dates as early as 1839, two years only after Chicago became an incorporated city, although the first public school under the school fund derived from the state grant of lands was started in 1834. In 1839 there were four teachers, but no regular school house. The city expended that year $1,600 for its schools. The High School was established by an ordinance of the City Council in 1855, and was first opened on the 8th of November, 1856. The edifice is located on Monroe street, near Halsted street, and cost $50,000.

From the report of the Board of Education we compile the following totals:

Universities and Colleges.

Population of city, April, 1868		242,873
Number entitled to attend schools		64,229
School districts—Grammar	21	
Primary	6—	27
Number of schools—High	1	
Grammar	21	
Primary	6—	28
Number of buildings—Owned	88	
Rented	11—	49
Having number of rooms		873
In which are employed:		
Male teachers	60	
Female teachers	341—	401
With enrolled pupils		29,954
With an average daily attendance of		17,658.1
The percentage of punctual attendance being		96.4
The ratio of all belonging in all the schools to the number of school age being		.286
The average number of pupils to a teacher being in—		
High School		32.4
Grammar Schools		47.0
Primary Schools		51.0
During the year there were:		
Suspensions for absence	2,946	
Suspensions for misconduct	3,921—	6,237
Cost per scholar for tuition upon average daily attendance		$15.71
Cost per scholar for incidentals		4.18
Cost per scholar for his share of valuation of school property		8.95
Annual cost per scholar		$28.84
Present number of seats in public schools		20,037
Number of pupils enrolled		20,879
Number awaiting seats		1,590
Number of private schools in school districts		118
With pupils Catholic	10,178	
Scandinavian and German	8,457	
Israelitish	303	
Other schools	8,780	
		17,718
Total receipts for fiscal year 1867—		
School tax	$387,486.99	
State fund	6,907.51	
Rents and interest	40,681.95	
		435,077.45
School construction bonds		298,158.76
Total receipts		$733,235.21
Total expenditures—		
From school tax fund	$349,145.25	
From school building fund	297,198.05	
		646,343.30
Balance of school fund on hand April, 1868		$130,159.51
The salaries of teachers amounted to		277,203.85

LITERARY AND SCIENTIFIC INSTITUTIONS.

THERE is every reason to believe that very soon the purely literary and scientific institutions of Chicago will be as conspicuous as is now its marvelous material growth. The centre of the commerce of the Mississippi Valley, and destined soon to control the wonderful mineral resources of the Far West, Chicago's higher mission is undoubtedly to become a centre of culture and refinement for the whole land. Indeed many of the most prominent merchants and capitalists of the city are already turning their thoughts towards the founding of such institutions as shall carry their names down to the latest posterity as wise and liberal promoters of the arts and sciences.

Among the more prominent of these is

THE ACADEMY OF SCIENCES,

located at No. 263 Wabash avenue, was established in 1857, and the formation of a Museum was then commenced, the labor of collecting being principally performed under the auspices of the Smithsonian Institute, by Major Robert Kennicott, who died in the early part of 1866, while engaged in an exploration of the then Russian America, since purchased by the United States. In 1865, Professor Agassiz being then delivering a course of lectures in Chicago, the occasion was seized upon to give a little more vitality to the institution, and funds were raised by the issuing of Life memberships of $500 each. The collections of the Society were removed to rooms in the Metropolitan Block, and there arranged pending the erection of the new building, now occupied by the Academy at No. 263 Wabash avenue, near Van Buren street. In 1866 the Metropolitan Block was burned, and the collections of the academy injured by fire, over eighteen thousand specimens being burned.

Literary and Scientific Institutions. 81

The new building, costing about $46,000, is 55 feet by 50, fire proof, and very strongly built, though plain in external appearance, as it will eventually form only an adjunct to a larger and finer building to be erected on the front of the lot, which is owned by the academy. The first two stories contain the library, work rooms, offices, etc., while the upper story forms the museum, which is twenty-eight feet high, and surrounded by two galleries. Dr. William Stimpson is secretary.

THE CHICAGO HISTORICAL SOCIETY

Is located on the corner of Ontario and North Dearborn streets. It was organized in 1856 with nineteen members, and chartered in the following year, occupying rooms in the Newberry block, on the corner of Wells and Kinzie streets. Under the management of Rev. Wm. Barry, the indefatigable secretary, the society amassed a rare collection of old books and manuscripts, with numerous valuable specimens, and incited to much original research into the natural and ethnological history of the northwest. The collection now numbers about 100,000 items, including 15,000 bound volumes; the society consists of about sixty active members; T. H. Armstrong secretary. A fire-proof building designed as a wing of a future edifice was erected in 1868 at a cost of about $35,000. The cost of the entire building when finished will be about $200,000. The building will have a frontage of one hundred and twenty feet on Ontario street, and one hundred and thirty-two feet on Dearborn, and will be sixty-six feet high from the sidewalk, besides a basement nine and one-half feet high. The first story will be eighteen feet high, and will contain a large entrance hall, a reading room, lecture room, office, museum, and binding and store-room. An open court will extend the whole height of the building, and be covered by a glass roof. This court will be 36x24 feet, and will be finished with smooth walls and marble floor, and is intended for the exhibition of statuary and other works of art.

THE CHICAGO LIBRARY ASSOCIATION,

Formerly the Young Men's Library, is in the hall on the corner of Randolph and LaSalle streets, generally known as Metropolitan Hall. The association derives its income from the annual fees of membership and proceeds of lectures. A movement is now progressing to accumulate a building fund for the erection of a suitable edifice which shall supply the present and future needs of the Association. In the rooms of the library may be found the latest files of all home and foreign newspapers and periodicals of merit.

UNION CATHOLIC LIBRARY ASSOCIATION

Is located at No. 122 LaSalle street. It was organized in 1868 by a few public spirited gentlemen, and is now in a very flourishing condition. It has a very excellently appointed reading room, and a well selected library of choice works, to which additions are being constantly made.

IRISH LITERARY ASSOCIATION.

This association meets in Blake's building, on Washington, near the corner of Wells street. It is yet in its infancy, having been organized in March, 1869. It is established on broad and liberal principles, independent of creed and sect, for the mutual, social, and literary advancement of its members.

LIBRARIES.

Chicago in her rapid advancement in material progress, has not altogether overlooked the advantages to be derived from well selected libraries. There are in the city many of the most valuable and extensive private collections in the country. Amongst the public libraries, that of the Law Institute is probably the most valuable. The libraries of her institutions of learning keep equal pace with their prosperity. That of the Historical Society is a very extensive collection. The next in prominence and value is that collected by the Young Men's Association, in Library Hall, corner of LaSalle and Randolph streets, now the Chicago Library Association.

The following is a list of the Public Libraries in the City:

LIBRARIES AND READING ROOMS.

Chicago Historical Society, Ontario, between Clark and Dearborn streets.
Chicago Law Institute, Third floor of Court House.
Free Library, N. Reuben st., near W. Chicago Ave.
Presbyterian Theological Seminary, Halsted street, cor. Fullerton Ave.
Chicago Library Association, Randolph, cor. LaSalle street.
Young Men's Christian Association, Madison, between Clark and LaSalle streets.
Union Catholic Library Association, 122 LaSalle street.

TELEGRAPH COMPANIES.

Western Union Telegraph Company — Office, northwest cor. Washington and LaSalle streets.

EXPRESS COMPANIES.

American Merchants Union Express Company — Office, 96 and 98 Lake street.
United States Express Company — Offices, 130 Lake, and 18 and 20 Clark street.

FOREIGN CONSULS IN CHICAGO.

Belgium — I. F. Henrotin, 110 N. LaSalle street.
Denmark (*Vice-Consul*) — P. Neils Peterson.
France (*Vice-Consul*) — Edmond Caney, residence 175 Lake street.
Great Britain — Francis Wilkins, acting consul, Office, 30 Reynolds Block.
Italy — August Fredin, residence 175 Lake street.
Netherlands (*Consular Agent*) — Henry S. Haas, Office, 161 Clark street.
Sweden and Norway — Peter L. Hawkinson, 2 Uhlich's Block.
Switzerland — Henry Enderis, 45 Clark street; Louis Borein, Vice-Consul.
North German Confederation — Henry Claussenius, 4 S. Clark street.

STEAMBOAT AND TRANSPORTATION COMPANIES.

American Transportation Company — Office, 19 Exchange Place.
Atlantic & Pacific Freight Express Line — Office, 41 Dearborn street.
Blue Line (*Through Freight*) — Office, 31 Dearborn street.
Buffalo, Cleveland & Chicago Line — 190 S. Water street.
Chicago & Green Bay Propeller Line — First Dock east of Rush street.
Chicago, Grand Haven & Muskegon, and Milwaukee, Port Washington, Sheboygan, Manitowoc & Two Rivers Line — First Dock east of Rush street Bridge.
Chicago & St. Joseph Line — Office, 4 and 6 River street.
Chicago & Grand Traverse Propeller Line — Office, Lumber street, cor. Maxwell.
Clary & Akhurst Line of Canal Boats — Office, Room 1, Steel's Buildings.
Empire Line — Office, 52 S. Clark street.

Evans' Buffalo & Chicago Line of Propellers — Office, Market street, between Washington and Madison.
Goodrich Transportation Company — Offices, on docks below Rush street bridge.
Grand Trunk Line and Lake Superior Line of Steamers — Office, S. Water st., foot of S. LaSalle street.
Grand Trunk Line of Propellers — Office, foot of LaSalle street.
Great Western Despatch Fast Freight Line — Offices, 130 Lake, and 20 Clark streets.
Lake Superior People's Line of Steamers — Office, Market st., between Washington and Madison.
Merchants Despatch Fast Freight Line — Office, 40 Dearborn street.
Michigan Canal & Illinois River Propeller Line — Office, foot of Wabash Ave.
Northern Transportation Company — Office, foot of N. LaSalle street.
Pittsburgh, Ft. Wayne & Chicago Fast Freight Line — Office, 65 Clark street.
Red Line Transit Company — Office, 54 Clark street.
Star Union Line — Office, 62 and 64 LaSalle street.
Stephens' St. Joseph, South Haven & Chicago Propeller Line — Office, 4 and 6 River street.
Union Despatch Company — Office, Monroe street, near State.
Western Express & People's Line — Office, S. Water st., foot of State.
Western States Line — Office, Market st., near Madison.
Western Transportation Company — Office, foot of State street.

NEWSPAPERS AND PUBLICATIONS.

The daily press of Chicago is universally acknowledged to be in ability and enterprise fully up to the metropolitan standard. There are now issued in Chicago three first-class daily morning papers in English, and two in German, and two evening papers. Each of the dailies issue a tri-weekly and weekly edition. There are eight daily publications of a miscellaneous character, and thirty weeklies, of which nine are specially devoted to religion, two of these in the German language, and one in the Swedish. There is one weekly printed in Italian, one in Scandivavian, two in the railroad interest, two spiritual, one insurance organ, and one to the Irish race, two agricultural, and one workingman's advocate. Of the sixteen monthlies three are religious, one of them being printed in the Swedish language, one is devoted to insurance, one to music, one to the order of Odd Fellows, and the balance of a miscellaneous order. There are ten monthly magazines, of which two are medical, (in addition to a quarterly medical issue) one is German, two Masonic, two religious and two literary, and one devoted to the advancement of the arts.

CHURCHES IN CHICAGO.

MANY of the church edifices in Chicago are of great elegance and beauty, and should not be overlooked by visitors who desire to see every thing in the city worth seeing. Our space does not admit of a detailed description, but we may be permitted to indicate a few of the most prominent and noteworthy. Christ, Grace, Trinity, St. James, and the Bishop's Church, Episcopal; The Church of the Holy Name, Holy Family, (Jesuit) and St. Joseph's (Catholic); First Baptist, Union Park Baptist, and Fifth Baptist; The New England and Plymouth, Congregational; Grace, Centenary and Wabash Avenue Methodist Episcopal; The First, Second, and Third Presbyterian; The First and Messiah Unitarian, and St. Paul's Universalist, are about the principal churches in architectural beauty.

The hours of divine service in nearly all the churches in Chicago are at $10\frac{1}{2}$ A.M. and $7\frac{1}{2}$ P.M. Sabbath-school at 2 P.M.

FIRST BAPTIST CHURCH.

LIST OF CHURCHES IN CHICAGO.

BAPTIST.

Bridgeport Baptist Church, Iron Clad Hall.
First Baptist Church, Wabash av., cor. Hubbard court.
First Danish Baptist Church, Union nr. W. Indiana st.
First German Baptist Church, Indiana, near Wood st.
Free Baptist Church, W. Jackson, cor. Peoria st.
Indiana Av. Baptist Church, Indiana av. cor. 13 st.
North Baptist Church, N. Dearborn, cor. Chicago av
Olivet Baptist Church, (colored) 4th av. nr. Taylor st.
Providence (col'd) Lecture Room Union Park Church.
Second Baptist Church, W. Monroe, S. W. cor. Morgan.
Second German Baptist, Chicago av., cor. Chase st.
Swedish Baptist Church, 110 Bremer st.
Union Park Baptist, W. Washington, cor. Paulina st.
Wabash Av. Baptist Church, Wabash av. cor. 18th st.
South Baptist Church, Boniface st., Bridgeport.
Fifth Baptist Church, Sangamon, cor. of Harrison.
North Star Mission, cor. Division and Sedgwick sts.
University Place Baptist Church.

CHRISTIAN CHURCH.

Christian Church, cor. Wabash av. and 16th sts.
Second Church, cor. Carpenter and Church sts.

CONGREGATIONAL.

First Church, W. Washington, cor. Green.
New England Church, White st., cor. N. Dearborn.
Plymouth Church, Wabash av., cor. Eldridge court.
Salem Church, Cleaverville.
South Church, Calumet av., N. E. cor. 26th st.
Tabernacle Church, cor. W. Indiana and N. Morgan st.
Union Park Church, Reuben, cor. W. Washington st.
Oakland Congregational Church, Lake, cor. Oakland av.
Bethany Church, cor. Paulina and 2nd sts.
Leavitt Street Church, W. Adams, cor. Leavitt st.
Lincoln Park, cor. Centre and Church sts.
North-West Mission Chapel, Milwaukee, cor. Western av.
Providence Mission, cor. Western av. and Warren av.

EPISCOPAL.

The Cathedral, cor. W. Washington and Peoria sts.
Calvary Church, Warren av. cor. Western av.
Christ Church, Michigan av., S E. cor. 24th st.
Church of the Ascension, cor. N. La Salle and Elm sts.
Church of the Holy Communion, Burnside st.
Grace Church, Wabash av. near 14th st.
St. Ansgarius, Indiana, cor. N. Franklin st.
St. John's Church, W. Lake st., cor. St. John's pl.
St. James' Church, cor. Cass and Huron sts.
St. Mark's Church, Cottage Grove.
St. Stephen's Church, Forquer, cor. Blue Island av.
Trinity Church, Jackson st., near Michigan av.
Church of the Epiphany, Throop, near W. Monroe st.
Church of the Atonement, Washington, cor. Robey st.
Church of Our Saviour, Belden, cor. Hurlbut st.
Cicero Mission Chapel, cor. Lake and Seymour sts.

EVANGELICAL ASSOCIATION OF NORTH AMERICA.

First Society, Polk st., cor. 3rd av.
Second Church, Chicago av., cor. Wells.
Third Church, W. 12th, S. W. cor. Union st.

GERMAN EVANGELICAL REFORMED.

First Church, Des Plaines, near Van Buren st.

EVANGELICAL LUTHERAN.

St. Paul's Church, Superior cor. N. Franklin.
Immanuel Church, W. Taylor, cor. Brown st.
Third, St. John's Church, 1st st., cor. Bickerdike.
Trinity Church, Hanover, cor. Kossuth st.

ENGLISH EVANGELICAL LUTHERAN.

First Church, Dearborn, north-east cor. Ontario st.

UNITED EVANGELICAL.

First German, St. Paul's, Ohio st., S. W. cor La Salle.
Fourth German, St. Peter's, Chicago av., cor. Noble st.
Zion Church, Union, N. W. cor. Mitchell st.
Third German, Salem Church, 21st st., cor. Archer ave.

INDEPENDENT.

Mission Church, Illinois st., bet. N. Wells and La Salle.

JEWISH CONGREGATIONS.

Church of the North Side, Superior, near Franklin st.
Sinai Congregation, Van Buren st., cor. 3d ave.
Kehilath Anshe Maarib, Wabash ave., cor. Peck ct.
Kehilath Benay Sholom, Harrison st., N. W. cor. 4th av.

METHODIST EPISCOPAL.

Simpson Street Church, Bonfield st., near St. Louis railroad.
Centenary Church, Monroe, bet. Morgan and Aberdeen sts
First Church, Clark, cor. Washington st.
First Scandinavian, Illinois, cor. Market st.
Free Methodist Church, Jefferson, near Polk st.
Grace Church, N. La Salle st., N. W. cor. Chicago ave.
Park Avenue Church, Park avenue, S. E. cor. Robey st.
Second Scandinavian, N. Sangamon, cor. 4th. st.
Trinity Church, 21st, cor. Indiana ave.
Wabash Avenue Church, cor. Harrison st.
West Indiana Church, cor. N. Sangamon st.
Wesley Chapel, Blackhawk, cor. Sedgwick st.
Grant Place Church, Larrabee st., cor. Grant Place.
Maxwell Street Church, between Newberry avenue and Johnson st.
Elston Road Church, Elston Road, cor. North ave.
Free M. E. Church, Morgan, bet. Lake and Fulton sts.
Indiana Avenue Church, between 32d and 33d sts.
African M. E. Church, 4th av., near Taylor st.
Illinois Chapel (African), Jackson st., cor. 4th av.

GERMAN METHODIST EPISCOPAL.

First German, 45, 47, and 49 Clybourne av.
West German Church, Maxwell, near Newberry st.
German Church, Van Buren, near Clark st.

LUTHERAN.

First Norwegian Evangelical, N. Franklin, cor. Erie st.
Our Saviour. Church, N. May, cor. W. Erie st.

Churches.

Swedish Evangelical Church, 190 and 192 Superior st.
The Evangelical Lutheran Church of the Unchanged Augsburg Confession, N. Peoria, cor. W. Indiana st.

PRESBYTERIAN—NEW SCHOOL.

Calvary Presbyterian Church, Indiana av., cor. 22d st.
First Hyde Park Church, Hyde Park.
First Presbyterian Church, Wabash av., near Van Buren st.
Eighth Presbyterian Church, Robey, cor. W. Washington street.
Ninth Presbyterian Church, Ellis av.
Olivet Church, Wabash av., cor. 14th st.
Second Presbyterian Church, Wabash av., cor. Washington st.
Seventh Presbyterian Church, Halsted, cor. Harrison st.
Third Presbyterian Church, Carpenter st., cor. W. Washington.
Thirty-first street Presbyterian Church, 31st st.
Welsh Church. Monroe, cor. Sangamon st.
Westminster Presbyterian Church, Ontario cor. N. Dearborn st.
Reformed Presbyterian Church, May, cor. Fulton st.

PRESBYTERIAN—OLD SCHOOL.

Fullerton Avenue Church, Fullerton av., near Clark st.
Jefferson Chapel, Adams, N. E. cor. Throop st.
North Presbyterian Church, Cass, S. E. cor. Indiana st.
South Presbyterian Church, Wabash av., nr. Congress.
Twenty-eighth St. Church, 28th st., near Wabash av.

PRESBYTERIAN—SCOTCH.

First Church, W. Adams, cor. Sangamon st.
Scotch Presbyterian Church, Peoria, near Monroe st.

PRESBYTERIAN—UNITED.

First United Presbyterian, Green, near W. Monroe st.
Third United Presbyterian, Superior, cor. N. Franklin.

REFORMED DUTCH.

First Church, Harrison, cor. May st.
American Reformed Church, W. Washington, nr. Ann.

ROMAN CATHOLIC.

Cathedral of the Holy Name, N. State st., cor. Superior.
Church of the Holy Family, West 12th, cor. May st.
Church of the Immaculate Conception, N. Franklin st.
Notre Dame de Chicago, Halsted, near Harrison st.
St. Bridget's Church, Bridgeport.
St. Boniface's Church, Cornell, N. E. cor. Noble st.
St. Columbkill Church, N. Paulina, cor. W. Indiana st.
St. Francis of Assissium, W. 12th st., cor. Newberry.
St. John's Church, Clark, cor. 18th st.
St. James' Church, Prairie av., bet. 26th and 27th sts.
St. Joseph's Church, Chicago av., N. E. cor. Cass st.
St. Louis' Church, Sherman, near Polk st.
St. Mary's Church, Wabash av., S. W. cor. Madison st.
St. Michael's, North av., cor. Church st.
St. Patrick's Church, S. Desplaines, N. W. cor. Adams.
St. Paul's, cor. Mather and Clinton sts.
St. Peter's, Clark, cor. Polk st.
St. Wenzeslaus, De Koven, N. E. cor. Desplaines st.

SWEDENBORGIAN.

Chicago Society of New Jerusalem, Adams, nr. State st.
German Society, Reuben st., near W. Chicago av.

UNITARIAN.

Church of the Messiah, Wabash av. cor. Hubbard ct.
Unity Church, cor. Dearborn and Whitney Sts.
All Souls, Ada, near Washington st.

UNIVERSALIST.

St. Paul's, Wabash av., cor. Van Buren st.
Church of the Redeemer, Sangamon, cor. Washington st.

CHRISTIAN CHURCH.

Christian Church, cor. Wabash av. and 16th st.
Second Church, cor. Carpenter and Front st.

QUAKERS.

Friends Meeting, 26th st., bet. Indiana and Prairie avs.

MISCELLANEOUS CHURCHES AND MISSIONS.

Church of God, cor. Warren av. and Robey st.
Christian Church, Indiana av. and 25th st.
Daily Noon Prayer Meeting, 148 and 150 Madison st.
Free Church, cor. Kankakee av. and 33rd st.
Advent Church, Monroe, bet. Clark and LaSalle sts.
Providence Mission, cor. Western and Warren avs.
Tammany Hall Mission, Lincoln, cor. Indiana sts.
Bremner Hall Mission, 340 N. Carpenter st.
Farwell Hall, Madison, bet. Clark and LaSalle sts.
Shields Mission, 21st st., cor. Wentworth av.
Outward Mission, Perch st., bet. Leavitt and Oakley.

From " Colbert's Chicago," already frequently quoted in this work, we take the following table:

RECAPITULATION.

These figures have been obtained in nearly every case from parties supposed to be good authority in the several denominations named, and some of them are doubtless liberal enough. The total Catholic attendance is probably of this character. A careful count would scarcely show a total attendance of 101,000 persons on any one Sunday of the year, in all the churches of the city, Catholic and Protestant. The following are the totals:

Denomination.	Churches.	Value.	Atten'e.	Scholars.
Roman Catholic	20	$8,543,000	101,617	15,700
Episcopal	12	747,500	5,850	2,900
Baptist	14	518,100	4,290	5,195
Methodist Episcopal	17	825,000	8,050	6,387
Presbyterian	19	1,069,500	6,850	8,525
Congregational	9	874,000	8,395	2,800
Unitarian	2	200,000	1,200	800
Universalist	2	185,000	1,450	840
Swedenborgian	3	85,000	265	180
Christian	2	18,000	270	190
Reformed	2	16,600	950	210
German, not above	11	860,000	5,800	1,600
Hebrew	4	105,000	367	235
Norwegian and Swedish Lutheran	4	51,000	2,000	925
Reformed Dutch	2	90,000	500	200
Other Societies	3	11,000	450	470
Totals	126	$8,203,100	148,117	41,557

REFORMATORY INSTITUTIONS

THE Chicago Reform School, pleasantly located a Cleaverville, on the lake shore, about two miles from the city, was opened November, 1856, for the reception and training of boys who were without the care o parents, or who, by vicious tendencies, needed specia care. The boys are instructed in the ordinary branche of a common English education, and are taught som useful trade.

THE INDUSTRIAL SCHOOL

On Archer road, near Brighton, was established in 186 by the late Very Rev. Dr. Dunne, under the auspices o the Society of St. Vincent de Paul, and is conducted b the Christian Brothers. Catholic parents, or guardian are permitted to choose this institution instead of th Reform School, where restraint is ordered by the court

THE WASHINGTONIAN HOME

Is located in the old Bull's Head Tavern on Madiso street, opposite Union Park. It was established for th reformation and cure of inebriates. Its support i derived from payments made by its inmates for boar and attendance, aided by liberal donations from th public spirited and charitable citizens, and also appro priations by the City Council. Until recently, it benefits have been confined to the male sex. A move ment is now on foot which will, no doubt, be successfu to extend its salutary benefits to unfortunate females.

THE ERRING WOMAN'S REFUGE

Is on Indiana avenue, a few doors south of Twenty fifth street, and as its name imports, is intended as home for penitent females who desire to be reclaime from a life of infamy. It is conducted under th auspices of an association of Protestant ladies who, in quiet and unostentatious manner, have accomplished

THE MAGDALEN ASYLUM,

large measure of good in a field where there is, unfortunately, still much to be done.

On the corner of Market and Hill streets, in the North Division, is under the charge of the Sisters of the Good Shepherd. It has been established for the reformation of fallen women. It was founded in 1858. In its early days the good sisters had to struggle against many hardships and great discouragements in carrying out their praiseworthy undertaking. At length, by the co-operation of the charitable citizens and the aid of Bishop Duggan, a half block of ground was purchased at a cost of $15,000, and a suitable building erected at an expense of $10,000. Several improvements have since been made, and the institution is now in a more prosperous condition. But, although much good has been done by the enterprise, the means at the disposal of the pious ladies is much too circumscribed, and appeals loudly to the benevolent for aid.

CHARITABLE INSTITUTIONS.

To enumerate each of the charitable institutions of the city would occupy more space than can be given in a little work of this kind. In addition to the corporate institution—the county poor house, situated in a healthy location, twelve miles north-west from the city—nearly all the churches have some association whose object is to relieve the necessitous. The St. Vincent de Paul society have a conference, composed of young men, in each of the Catholic churches, and in an unostentatious manner visit the sick and relieve the poor constantly and systematically. The Young Men's Christian Association, the Association of the Ministry at Large, and the City Relief and Aid Society, in like manner, do a world of good.

THE PROTESTANT ORPHAN ASYLUM

Is located on Michigan avenue, corner of Twenty-second street. It is a noble charity, admirably conducted, and has over four hundred homeless little waifs, both girls and boys, who are tenderly cared for, and trained for a life of usefulness.

HOME FOR THE FRIENDLESS.

This institution occupies a three-story brick building, at 911 Wabash avenue. It is supported entirely by voluntary contributions. A large sum is thus collected, and annually expended in providing for the comfort and protection of numbers of homeless and friendless poor, principally children, who are being constantly received, and provided with homes in charitable families.

THE OLD LADIES HOME

Is located in a building owned by the Association, on Indiana avenue, near Twenty-seventh street. In this institution many respectable and worthy old ladies find a home, who, otherwise, would be left to the cold charities of the world, and suffer many bitter hardships. This is is one of the very noblest charities of the city, and is eminently deserving of support.

NURSERY AND HALF ORPHAN ASYLUM

Is located on the corner of Wisconsin and Franklin streets.

ST. JOSEPH'S MALE ORPHAN ASYLUM,

No. 267 Wabash avenue, under charge of the Sisters of Mercy.

ST. MARY AND ST. JOSEPH'S ORPHAN ASYLUM

Corner of Superior and N. State street, under the charge of the Sisters of St. Joseph.

PROTESTANT ORPHAN ASYLUM,

Michigan avenue, cor. Twenty-second street.

HOSPITALS AND DISPENSARIES.

COOK COUNTY HOSPITAL

Is located in a commodious and elegant four-story brick building on Arnold, between Eighteenth and Nineteenth streets.

MERCY HOSPITAL

Is located on Calumet Avenue between Twenty-fifth and Twenty-sixth streets. It is under the charge of the Sisters of Mercy.

ST. LUKE'S FREE HOSPITAL.

Occupies a beautiful brick edifice at No. 669 State street. It is under the immediate auspices of the Protestant Episcopal congregations of the city.

THE SMALL-POX HOSPITAL

Occupies a beautiful and salubrious site on North Avenue near the lake shore. It is under the charge of the municipal Board of Health.

HOSPITAL FOR WOMEN AND CHILDREN

Is located at No. 94 Rush street.

PROTESTANT DEACONESS HOSPITAL

Is located at No. 141 North Dearborn street.

ST. MARY'S HOSPITAL

Is located at No. 527 North Dearborn street, conducted by the Alexian Brothers. It is free to those who can not afford to pay for services.

UNITED STATES MARINE HOSPITAL.

Michigan Avenue near Rush street Bridge.

MEDICAL AND ELECTRICAL INSTITUTE,

Established in 1862, for the treatment and cure of chronic diseases, at 189 Wabash avenue. We have succeeded in establishing a place where home comforts can be enjoyed by the invalid in a house of modern improvements, in a central locality on beautiful Wabash avenue. Our table is furnished with the best bread, meats, vegetables and fruits the market affords. Patients advised what course of diet is best in each individual case.

Patients calling for examination and prescription or Medical Electrical treatment are not generally detained an hour, unless their case is a critical one. There are diseases that we do not treat; a letter of inquiry will be promptly answered if a return stamp is inclosed, and if your case is one that we do not treat, we will direct you to the best physicians in our city, which may save you from paying an exorbitant fee in advance, and being unmercifully quacked by a brazen-faced charlatan.

We hold no secret remedies; physicians are always welcome to an examination of our Medical and Electrical means. No one remedy is used to the exclusion of all others. The system of practice is to meet the exigency of the case with an appropriate remedy, which science and experience have furnished for the relief or cure of the suffering invalid.

The Medical and Electrical means are very elaborate and complete. The *electrical iron bath*, as improved by Mr. Varley, of London, is *par excellence* as a tonic in general debility, and in all cases where iron is indicated. The Electro-Thermal Bath we AVER to be superior to any yet invented as to facility in changing and directing the currents, and is one of the most efficacious baths in use,—its power in removing *colds, arresting local congestions, equalizing the circulation, tranquilizing the nervous system and giving immediate relief to the over-wrought, brain, is not surpassed by any other bath.*

Prominent among the diseases treated are: Nervous Diseases, Palsy, Neuralgia, Rheumatism, Scrofula, General Debility, Diseases of the Lungs and Heart Catarrh and Bronchitis, Liver, Spleen and Kidneys, and Diseases of WOMEN and CHILDREN.

CHICAGO HOTEL FOR INVALIDS.

All that modern science and art could suggest, has been employed to render this institution the most perfect of its kind in the country. The advantages it offers to those needing medical services, are as follows:

While it has all the comforts and elegance of a first-class hotel, yet it is strictly private and free from all the disturbances so detrimental to the recovery of invalids, while stopping at public resorts. The rooms are spacious, neatly furnished and thoroughly ventilated. Experienced nurses are in attendance day and night. Each patient occupies a private apartment, and is as much isolated, if desired, as if the only occupant of the institution. The Lying-in department is complete in all its appointments, with competent female nurses. Charges reasonable, giving persons of moderate means the privilege of availing themselves of the benefits of the institution. Patients, if they so desire, may select their own physician. All classes of diseases and disabilities will be received that are not contagious, the latter being strictly prohibited. All communications must be addressed to the surgeon or physician, 249 and 251 South Clark street.

DISPENSARIES.

For affording gratuitous medical treatment to out-door indigent patients.

THE CHICAGO CITY DISPENSARY

Is located on State street two doors north of Twenty-second street, and is in immediate connection with the Chicago Medical College.

CHARITY DISPENSARY,

On North Dearborn, corner of Indiana street. In connection with Rush Medical College. It is open every day from 3 to 4 P.M. Patients are prescribed for free of charge, and when unable to visit the Dispensary are visited at their homes.

Hospitals and Dispensaries.

HAHNEMANN COLLEGE DISPENSARY

Is at No. 168 South Clark street. Open every day for the medical and surgical treatment of the sick poor.

THE CHICAGO CHARITABLE EYE AND EAR DISPENSARY

Is at No. 16 East Pearson street, in the North Division of the city, and is open every day from 2 to 3 P. M. for the gratuitous treatment of the sick poor who are afflicted with diseases of the eye and ear.

FREE HOMŒOPATHIC DISPENSARY

Is at 240 West Madison street, open from 1 to 2 each day, (Sundays excepted).

CHICAGO EYE AND EAR INFIRMARY, Reynold's Block, corner Dearborn and Madison streets, B. P. Reynolds, M. D., surgeon in charge, successfully treats all curable diseases of the eye and ear, and skillfully performs every operation connected with ophthalmic and aural surgery. French artificial eyes and ear drums, etc., inserted, Dr. Reynolds has recently published the following new works: "The Eye and Ear. Their Diseases and Means of Cure," with twenty engravings. Price, bound in cloth, $2.50. "Head, Throat, and Lungs," with ten engravings. Bound in cloth, $1. "Discourses on Important Subjects." Bound in cloth, $2. "The Will of Man." Bound in cloth, $1. "Chicago Journal of Health," edited by Dr. Reynolds. Published monthly. Price, $1 per year; single numbers, 10 cents. Published by Western News Company.

PUBLIC BUILDINGS.

THE COURT HOUSE

Is a building of stately proportions, now in course of enlargement, by the addition of two wings on the east and west sides, which will make the building extend clear from Clark to LaSalle streets. It is built of limestone brought from Lockport, New York, before it was discovered that the State of Illinois could furnish a superior stone from her own bosom.

In this building are located the various city and county courts, the officers of the municipal and county governments, and the county jail. The tower, which is two hundred feet above the level of the streets, is approached by a winding staircase, and affords the loftiest standpoint from which the visitor can obtain a magnificent view of the city and lake.

THE POST OFFICE AND CUSTOM HOUSE

Is located on the corner of Dearborn and Monroe streets. This imposing structure is one of the finest, as it has been one of the most costly public buildings in Chicago. It is built of Athens marble and iron, and is perfectly fire-proof. The Post Office department occupies the entire of the first floor, and part of the basement and second floor. The Custom House and offices of Internal Revenue, are located on the second floor, and the United States Circuit and District Courts, and the United States Marshall and District Attorney the third floor.

CHAMBER OF COMMERCE—BOARD OF TRADE

Is located on the corner of Washington and LaSalle streets. Its walls are built of Athens marble, and its dimensions are 93 by 181 feet. It is in the modern Italian style of architecture, and consists of a basement, half beneath the street, and used for business offices; a story above, occupied by banks, insurance and commission offices; and above this the grand hall, where the members of the Board of Trade assemble daily.

The building is surmounted by a Mansard roof, pierced with oval windows, the corners ornamented with urns. The entrance consists of four handsome Corinthian columns, from which spring three arches supporting a handsome balcony, underneath which a broad flight of stairs leads to the first floor. On the whole, the structure has an imposing appearance. The building and the ground upon which it is situated cost $400,000. The property is in the hands of a joint-stock company, and the rents derived from the various offices afford remunerative dividends. The completion of the building was celebrated by grand and appropriate festivities, on the 30th and 31st of August, 1865, which were attended by delegations from all the principal cities of the Union and Canadas.

No visitor can "do" Chicago without entering the grand hall during 'Change hours, which are from 11 A.M. to 1 P.M. The balcony overlooking the busy scene in the hall below is open to strangers, and during the busy periods of the year presents a spectacle which is well worth a long journey to witness.

THE NEW TRIBUNE BUILDING

Is, in every respect, a model of beauty, convenience and comfort, and an ornament to the city. It is located on the corner of Madison and Dearborn streets. It fronts 72 feet on Dearborn, by 121 feet on Madison street, and covers an area of 8,712 square feet. The

CHICAGO TRIBUNE BUILDING

building is constructed entirely of fire proof materials. It is four stories high above the basement, with a complete altitude of 70 feet. The entire building is heated by steam, with radiators in every room. Ventilating flues near the floor are also constructed in every room. Especial pains have been taken to make the ventilation perfect in every respect. The style of architecture is "Roman," which allows great diversity of detail and ornamentation. Both street fronts are of Athens marble, from the sidewalk to the cornice. The cornices are of galvanized iron, artistically and elaborately finished, with pediments, parapets, etc. The total cost of the building has been about $200,000.

THE FIRST NATIONAL BANK BUILDING.

Among the fine public buildings which have merits sufficient to challenge bold and outspoken criticism, this edifice, with Potter Palmer's block across the way, ranks first. The building is 75 by 80, thoroughly fire-proof in construction, and cost the sum of $180,000. Every thing about it has been done for permanence, and perhaps, in this respect, it represents the idea of truth in architecture as well as any other building we have in Chicago. The foundations are apparent; broad, massive, significant of carrying power, while the superstructure is equally as impressive of strength. There is no attempt at useless ornamentation by way of French frippery and unmeaning symbols. The architect evidently had in view the advantage to be obtained in the general effect by depth of shadow, which the liberal policy pursued by the officers of the First National Bank allowed him to carry into execution to his satisfaction. In the estimation of that portion of the public who look at architecture from a critical standpoint, whether as amateurs or professionals, this building is almost universally regarded as among the finest and most imposing in the country.

MERCHANTS INSURANCE COMPANY
BUILDING.

THE MERCHANTS INSURANCE COMPANY BUILDING.

One of the most stately and beautiful edifices in the United States, is the new building of the Merchants Insurance company of Chicago, on the northwest corner of LaSalle and Washington streets. It is five stories in height, and has a frontage of ninety-six and one-third feet on LaSalle street, and a frontage of one hundred and eleven and a half feet on Washington street. Both the front elevations are built of magnesian limestone, from Athens, of which so many of our best buildings are made. The total height of the structure, from the sidewalk to the cornice, is eighty-two and a half feet. The style of the architecture is the modified Italian, such variations having been made as are necessary to adapt it to the rigor of our climate. The LaSalle street elevation, fronting the court house, being most conspicuous, is therefore most elaborate in its workmanship and ornamentation. For the French roof style has been substituted a more classic, and truly American architecture. The ornamentation is, to a considerable degree, original, the carved flowers, fruits and leaves being generally selected from native American plants. The interior of the first and second stories is wainscotted with black walnut, in neat and tasteful panels, after the French style. The second story floor is laid with alternate dark and light colored marble tiles, and from the centre of this floor rises the stairway to the several stories above. This stairway, with its landings, occupies considerable space in the exact centre of the building; and on each floor, all the rooms open into the square hall which encloses the stairway. Two large and elaborate entrances lead to the main hall from LaSalle street, and one from Washington street. The first and second stories are finished in hard wood, and all the glass for the interior, as well as the exterior of these stories, is the best French plate.

The black walnut railing and balustrades of the stairway are particularly noticeable for their massiveness and elegance of structure. The stairways rest on iron carriages.

The building is heated throughout with steam, and in its ventilation, the latest and most improved methods have been employed. The roof is of extra thickness, and is constructed of Barrill's composition. The building cost about $300,000.

THE DOUGLAS MONUMENT.

At Cottage Grove, on the lake shore, stands the monument of Senator Douglas. The grave and monument may be easily reached by the Cottage Grove horse-cars. The ride will occupy but a few minutes, and the visitor will be amply paid for his trouble.

BANKING IN CHICAGO.

Until the passage of the national banking act of 1864 the business of banking in Chicago was subject to many fluctuations and serious derangements. It was not until 1864 that the era of true banking began. During that year seven national banks were organized, with an aggregate capital of about $3,000,000. There are now thirteen national banks in this city, with an aggregate capital of $7,450,000.

In addition to the thirteen national banks, there are in Chicago several private banking establishments, controlled by gentlemen of large capital, financial skill, and stainless integrity. Among these we may, without invidious distinction, enumerate the old established and prosperous house of Henry Greenebaum & Co., W. P. Vandursen & Co., connected with the well known New York house of Swann & Payson; also the firm of Geo. C. Smith & Brother, well and favorably known in financial circles.

CHICAGO CLEARING HOUSE.

During the year 1865 it was deemed necessary to establish a clearing house, similar to that which had been found to promote the convenience and safety of

banking in New York. A charter was granted by the Legislature, and the Chicago Clearing House commenced business on the 6th of April, 1865. The affairs of the association have been skillfully and carefully conducted, and the banks composing it have derived great benefit therefrom. The total clearings during its first year's operations amounted to $449,710,435; from the 1st of January, 1868, to the 31st of December, 1868, it amounted to $718,485,908.39.

SAVINGS BANKS.

The first savings bank in the city was established in 1857. These institutions have always maintained a high credit through all the vicissitudes of "wild cat" and war times, which caused so many private banking houses to succumb, and so completely revolutionized the banking system of the country. We give a view of the building occupied by the Merchants', Farmers and Mechanics' Savings Bank, No. 13 Clark street. This institution was chartered in 1861, and in 1864 removed to its present very appropriate and convenient edifice. The institution is in a highly flourishing condition, and is deservedly popular. Interest is allowed on sums of five dollars and upwards, and is paid semi-annually, on the first day of January and the first day of July. The system of keeping accounts and receiving and paying money, and also as to the investment of the same, is similar to that so long and so successfully pursued by the best savings banks in New York and New England. A popular feature of this bank is, that married women and minors are allowed to deposit funds in their own name, thus placing them beyond the reach of husbands, parents, or guardians.

The business of this institution is confined *exclusively* to the receipt and care of savings deposits, and funds deposited in trust. No commercial or general banking business is transacted.

MERCHANTS' FARMERS', AND MECHANICS'
SAVINGS BANK.

A certain proportion of the funds are invested by loan upon real estate in the city of Chicago. In making such loans preference is always given to applications from depositors of small means, who have accumulated in the institution sufficient funds to pay for a lot of ground, and desire to borrow something more to aid them in erecting buildings to be used as permanent homes for themselves and families.

THE HIBERNIAN BANKING ASSOCIATION.

This popular institution is located on the south-west corner of Lake and Clark streets. Its officers are gentlemen of large experience in banking, and the directors include some of our most successful merchants, whose financial ability is amply attested by the success which has attended them in their own business. Besides the savings department, the bank transacts a general commercial, banking and foreign exchange business.

INSURANCE COMPANIES.

UNTIL within the last few years, the business of Insurance in Chicago was mainly conducted by agencies representing companies outside this city and State. In 1865, after the close of the war, however, the merchants and capitalists of Chicago began to appreciate the importance and magnitude of the field presented to them in this line, and before the end of that year fourteen fire and marine, one life, and two accident companies were organized, of which the citizens of Chicago were the stockholders. There are now 22 Chicago companies, including 16 fire, 5 life, and one life and accident. There are also in the city 40 agents for fire companies, 60 life insurance companies, two live stock, one railroad accident, one steam boiler, and three general accident companies represented. Of the Chicago companies, one dates from 1853, and was reorganized in 1864, four were organized in 1855, one in 1859, one in 1861, three in 1863, four in 1865, four in 1866, one in 1867, and three in 1868. Their aggregate capital is about eight million dollars. The rate of insurance on fire now averages about 2¼ per cent.

MERCHANTS INSURANCE COMPANY OF CHICAGO.

The business edifice just completed by this company on the corner of LaSalle and Washington streets, is a grand achievement. A description and illustration of which appears under the heading of Public Buildings.

The Charter of the Merchants Insurance Company was obtained and held by the Mercantile Association of Chicago. During the winter sessions of the association in 1862-3, it was decided to place the charter and the advantages of organization of an insurance company before the mercantile interests of the city. The association held this charter until the early spring of 1863, when Wm. E. Doggett, Wm. McKindley, George Armour, John V. Farwell, John Tyrrell, Merrill Ladd, and others in the interest of the association canvassed the street, and the requisite amount of stock was subscribed without delay, and in June 1863 the Merchants Insurance Company proceeded to business, and from its inception to the present time the company has grown in favor and to its present collossal proportions. At this early day fire insurance in Chicago was but a feeble success. We had but one successful company, and the undertaking was canvassed at the sessions of the association. The trying days of war naturally made men of means and influence timid, but the association disposed of the charter and the company commenced business under the guidance and personal supervision of Wm. E. Rollo, who, to the present day, has led the company from small beginnings to its present proud and prominent position among the sterling companies of the country. The progress of the company, under his able management, excels that of any western, and a large majority of eastern companies. The Merchants has steadily grown in financial strength. The capital stock of the company has not only increased by assessment, but largely by dividends; and in no instance has the stock of the company necessarily been thrown upon the market for sale at a sacrifice to the holder. A market has at all times been found, at its full value, and is now above par. One of the most striking illustrations of the secretary's farsighted wisdom was the union effected, by which the capital and business influence of the Packers and Provision Dealers Insurance Company was secured to the interests of the Merchants, and still more recently the consolidation of the capital and risks of the Traders Insurance Company. Its present cash capital is five hundred thousand dollars, and surplus about a quarter of a million dollars.

COMMERCIAL INSURANCE COMPANY.

We have become so accustomed to look eastward for successful and reliable insurance companies, that we often overlook those at our own doors, which, in all the essentials of solvency, are the peers of any in the land. Among these the Commercial Insurance Company, of this city, occupies an eminent position, alike for the care with which it is managed, and the security which it affords to its insured. This company was organized in 1865 by some of our most responsible business men, and entered upon its work at a time when there was little in the immediate past or future of fire insurance to attract capital to the venture, or promise even ordinary return for the money invested. But the men who organized and controlled the "Commercial" were not of ordinary mould. They did not embark in the enterprise without careful study of the charts which experience had provided, and the requisite judgment and firmness to avoid the dangers which had proved fatal to other voyagers. As the result of their energy and skill we have a company possessed of assets to the amount of $334,175.59, of which all, save $135,000 of stock notes, amply guaranteed, is in cash or its equivalent. Of this amount, there is held real estate to the value, at a moderate valuation, of $140,000, which pays an annual rental of $17,000. Upon

Insurance Companies.

160 & 162 WASHINGTON ST.
CHICAGO.

Insurance Companies.

this is erected the magnificent building of the company, at Nos. 160 and 162 Washington street, the solid marble walls of which are emblematical of its strength, and the beauty of whose presence, contrasted with the unsightliness of the location a few years ago, fitly typifies the wonderful progress which the "Commercial" has made within that time.

Counting the value of this real estate alone, and excluding from the calculation *all* its other assets, the "Commercial" is possessed of a much larger percentage of assets to risk in force than the average of Fire Insurance Companies reporting to the New York Insurance Department.

During the four years of its existence the losses of the "Commercial" (fire and marine) have been but 46 per cent. of its premium receipts, a ratio which is less than the average of American companies for the same time, and is in itself the best possible proof of careful and successful management. During the same period it has paid 35 per cent. of dividends upon its capital stock, thus demonstrating that Western brain and energy can make even the unpromising venture of fire and marine insurance lucrative and safe.

Of the men into whose hands its fortunes have been from the first committed, the above facts speak more approvingly than words. Mr. J. C. Dore, the President, is well and widely known as a gentleman of culture, ability, and integrity. Mr. Jefferson Farmer, the Secretary, is an efficient, skillful, and successful underwriter, of fifteen years experience in the business, whose merit is acknowledged wherever in the West the science of underwriting is known, and to whose fidelity, ability, and devotion is mainly due the success of the "Commercial." The Board of Directors comprises some of our best known and most reliable citizens, whose reputations have been honestly earned by long years of fair dealing and successful business enterprise, and whose names are a tower of strength to any institution fortunate enough to obtain them.

Hitherto the "Commercial" has done no agency business. They are now about organizing an extended agency system, and we are proud to commend the company and its officers to every community throughout the West, as eminently worthy of confidence, and fully able and willing to make good all their obligations.

CHICAGO FIREMENS INSURANCE COMPANY.

The removal of this company from its former location on Lake street to No. 92 La Salle street, in the north end of the basement of the Merchants Insurance Company's building, furnishes fit occasion for a short review of its past record, and its present claims upon the confidence and patronage of the public.

That record, if it is not signalized by any great or daring exploit on the perilous field of fire underwriting, is unsullied by a single act of unfair dealing with its insured, or a single failure to fulfill its contracts to the letter. Organized in 1855, it has, for the fourteen years of its existence, been managed with peculiar caution—doing no agency business, and taking no risks except over its own counter, and under the personal supervision of its own officers. During that time it has paid losses to the amount of nearly $500,000, and of these only one under the compulsion of a legal judgment against the company. In the settlement of claims, the Chicago "Firemens" have been accustomed to regard first, last, and always, the equities of the case, exceeding often in their performances the literal promises of the contract. When the loss was clearly an honest one, and the claim just, prompt settlement has been considered a duty, and the record of losses paid shows that, in such cases, the average delay before payment has not been over thirty days.

In such a course as this, as jealously guarding the fortunes of the company as the rights of the insured, the Chicago "Firemens" has been rewarded with a steady and healthful growth. Its present assets are $320,000, of which $200,000 is invested in United States five twenty bonds. Its premium receipts for the year 1868 were $160,000, and on these its losses were *forty-five per cent. less* than the average losses of the companies reporting to the New York State Insurance

FIRST NATIONAL BANK BUILDING.

Department. This is not because of any rapid accession of new business, the term of insurance upon which has but just begun; for the amount insured April 1, 1868 was increased, on April 1, 1869, by only four per cent.

We doubt if many companies can successfully compete with the Chicago "Firemens" in economy of management. In 1868 its entire expenses, including salaries, commissions, and taxes, were but 16¾ per cent. of the premium receipts, and only 15 per cent. of the total income, and of these expenses the commissions paid for business were only 6¾ per cent. of premium receipts, or 4 per cent. of the total income. It is little matter of surprise to learn that a company so managed has paid, since January 1, 1864, an average cash dividend to its stockholders of 14 per cent.

Of its directors and officers little need be said. They are all of them gentlemen well known to our business community, and known only to be respected as capable and honest men. Their capacity and integrity have made the Chicago "Firemens" what it is to-day, a success, none the less praiseworthy and enduring because it has been achieved in the quiet pursuit of daily duty, and without boastful blazonry of itself.

PUTNAM FIRE INSURANCE COMPANY.

"They are not all Israel who are of Israel," and the Putnam Fire Insurance Company, of Hartford, have not inherited the mad-cap impetuosity of the redoubtable hero who, as tradition tells us, crawled out on the rotten limb in search of bird's eggs, made the desperate venture of the wolves' den, and later, rode down Horse-Neck, at the imminent risk of his own neck.

If, however, they fail of his reckless daring, they are the inheritors of his sterling integrity, and in their career have made a record no less proud, although more peaceful, than that of the immortal Israel himself.

This company was organized at Hartford, Conn., in June, 1864, by men who thoroughly understood both the hazards and principles of fire underwriting. Its capital was $500,000, ample enough to secure its

patrons against prospective loss, and to assure them of
the good faith and firm determination of those who
essayed the venture.

From that time onward its history has been the history of careful management and scrupulous integrity,
devoted to the prosecution of a business whose natural
hazards were abnormally increased by the vicissitudes
of the time, and which demands for its successful conduct those qualities in the highest degree.

Throughout the storm of fire which, for the last five
years, has beat upon all our companies with unexampled fury, those qualities in its management have stood
the "Putnam" in good stead, and it is by virtue of
them alone that the company has endured, fulfilling
all its contracts, and retaining always the explicit confidence of a public quick to recognize and appreciate
true merit, whenever it is found.

Such has been its management, that to-day it presents itself with an unimpaired capital and assets of
over $659,000, and a record on which there is no stain
of dishonor.

Forward to catch the spirit and join the onward
movement of the times, it has, for the better accomodation of its Western patrons and the greater security
of its business, established a western branch office in
this city, at rooms Nos. 16 and 17 Merchants Insurance Company's building, corner of La Salle and
Washington streets, to which office, agents in the States
of Ohio, Indiana, Illinois, Michigan, Wisconsin, Minnesota, Iowa, Missouri, Kansas, Nebraska, and Kentucky will henceforth make their daily reports of risks,
renewals, endorsements, changes, applications, surveys, and diagrams of special hazards, letters of inquiry
relative to rates and practice; and also their regular
reports and remittances.

This office is under the management of Robert J.
Smith, Esq., a gentleman well known throughout the
West as an experienced underwriter, and whose previous success as a general agent of this company is the
ample guarantee of his fitness for his new and responsible position. In thus identifying itself with Western
interests, and becoming one of us, the "Putnam" has

not only exhibited its usual foresight and shrewdness, but strengthened its already strong claims upon our confidence and patronage. We are glad of the occasion which this action of the "Putnam's" gives us to commend it and its officers, as we do without hesitation and reserve, to our insuring public. It may not dazzle, as its namesake did, by deeds of splendid daring, but, like him, it will be found in every emergency "steadfast and true."

THE WASHINGTON LIFE.

The Washington Life Insurance Company of New York, and its success, gives us the opportunity in this connection, of placing the western agency equally prominent with the Merchants and *its* success, and, in a measure, enjoying with it the most prominent business location in Chicago; in fact, the Washington Life towers above its *lessor*. We well remember Paul & Mason in their little seven by nine room, when they first accepted the agency of the company in the spring of 1865. The company, then in its fifth year, had little or no reputation outside of New York city. The company had but 2,550 policies in force at the end of the year, having written but 1,106 policies during the year 1865, with assets of only $500,000. The Washington Life and its management fully appreciated the demands of the west, and knowing they had in their western agents men of integrity and consummate business qualifications, left nothing undone to aid them in placing the Washington in the front ranks of life insurance companies in the west. In the short space of four years the Washington Life has become as widely known as the great founder of our republic, and like him, is a general favorite. The Washington Life, in fact, is a great public favorite, and its fame for honorable dealing is as wide spread as its name is national. Its business since 1865, has been a prosperous one, and in no one year do we find so large an increase as the year 1868. The Washington Life is the only New York company, with one exception, that shows an increase of policies issued, exceeding two thousand in number, and its losses and expenses compare very favorably with any other company of the same age. In 1868 the company issued 5,089 policies, insuring $10,804,570, having in all 8,885 policies in force, insuring $20,355,035, with a capital and accumulations at this date, of nearly $2,000,000; thus, within four years after its president, Cyrus Curtiss, with his usual sagacity, saw in the west the elements of greatness, the Washington Life stands a proud monument of his skill and shrewd foresight in placing his company's interests and destiny in the hands of agents of sterling worth and progressive activity. It is the progressive activity of Paul & Mason that enables the Merchants Insurance Company to have for its permanent lessee the Washington Life Insurance Company, whose business has compelled its agents to seek their new and commodious quarters. The growing business of the company in Chicago and the west has demanded for a year past enlarged facilities in the centre of business, and not until the plans of the Merchants building were made and decided upon did the agents of the Washington know where they could secure the proper location with the necessary facilities for conducting their rapidly growing business. In the occupancy of that portion of the Merchants building, on the floor immediately above the office of the Western Union Telegraph Company, the most ample accommodations are secured, fronting on LaSalle as well as Washington street. The Washington Life is not only a great public favorite, but its western agency is making it a great public benefactor, and in its new and commodious quarters fitted up in a most elaborate style, makes it a great public convenience for business, which, with its superior inducements, will necessarily add to its already large and rapidly increasing income.

THE NEW PHŒNIX BUILDING.

Among the many business edifices that adorn our city the new Phœnix Insurance Building, 90 La Salle street, holds a distinguished place. The structure stands four feet high, exclusive of basement, and has a front of white marble, which presents an aspect at once chaste and magnificent. The emblematic bird, in golden glory, surmounts the roof, and his extended wings seem spread invitingly to welcome property owners beneath their protection.

The office of the Company, situated on the first floor, is a marvel of elegance and comfort. The furniture, which is of the finest quality of black walnut, inlaid and panelled with French walnut of the best texture and polish, is beautiful in design and workmanship. Each of the desks is surmounted by a golden phœnix, and graven with the company monogram, which is also exquisitely painted on the windows of the office.

The Phœnix Insurance Company, of Hartford, is long and popularly known, and its business reputation is so thoroughly established, that there is no necessity for extravagant encomiums. Suffice it to say, that in its dealings with the insured it has ever been just and liberal. The Phœnix was organized in 1854, with a cash capital of $200,000, and its assets now amount to more than a million and a half of dollars, of which above $250,000 is net surplus, and its stock sells at a higher premium than that of any of the other fire insurance companies of Hartford. Considering the financial standing and splendid record of the Phœnix, we may justly class it among the most successful business enterprises of the United States.

It is ably represented here by Henry H. Brown, Esq., who is also the representative of several other large companies. To the great success of the Phœnix the Chicago agency has contributed in no small degree; and to those who are desirous of being insured (and what owner of property is not?) no fairer or more reliable inducements can elsewhere be given.

THE HOME INSURANCE COMPANY OF CHICAGO.

This company commenced business in February of last year. Among its officers, directors, and stockholders we recognize the names of many of the "oldest inhabitants," whose reputation for strict integrity and honorable dealing, acquired from many years of successful individual enterprise, was sufficient to make it a matter of certainty, that the company would soon gain the confidence of the public, and that its real worth would meet with the abundant success which it merited.

Skill and prudence in the management of the company's affairs were guaranteed by the appointment of its experienced secretary, Mr. Thomas Buckley. The capital of the company is $200,000, and the net profits for the eleven months of last year amounted to $22,732.27, making the assets of the company January 1st, 1869, $222,731.37. These assets are in cash, government bonds, and bonds and mortgages on choice real estate. The business of the company during the six months of this year exhibits a large increase, and the excellent standing and gratifying progress which the company has achieved entitle it to the enviable position which it has taken, as one of Chicago's favorite companies; and such is its merit and stability, that a policy in the "Home of Chicago" is considered "as good as the gold."

THE REPUBLIC INSURANCE COMPANY.

"Facts are stubborn things." They will neither be reasoned nor ridiculed down. Rhetoric can not master them, nor speculation prevail against them. The success of the Republic Insurance Company, of this city, is an established fact; its assets of $1,293,018.49, of which $1,029,455 is in United States bonds, are facts, and, if we may judge by the amount of painful effort and shameless misrepresentation employed to overcome them, *ugly* facts for those who, at the organization of this company, filled the land with their prophecies of failure, and have since busied themselves to secure the fulfillment of those prophecies.

The logic of those who attempt to reason down the "Republic" is equally at fault. Thus we have one insurance journal, itself a thing of yesterday, assuming to sit in judgment upon the monthly statements of this company, and gravely reasoning that these can not be true, because they show a greater monthly gain of

Insurance Companies. 121

surplus than the entire net monthly premium receipts! Did not the young Daniel, who thus comes to judgment, know that the gain of the "Republic" for the past month, in the single item of appreciation of bonds, was no less than $33,050—that, during the same period, $106,200 of its capital stock was taken and paid for at $25 per share of $100, $5 per share of which was premium? These two sources alone give a total gain of $38,300 for the month. If he did not know these facts his ignorance abundantly qualifies him to keep silence. If he knew them, and found it necessary, for the purpose of his argument, to ignore them, the readiness with which he did so abundantly testifies to the character of his motive.

Such unavailing attempts to decry the Republic Insurance Company only serve to bring out in bold relief the strength of its position, and the weakness of its adversaries.

The fact is, that no Insurance Company in the United States is more cautiously and ably managed. In none is the entire procedure of the officers subjected to a scrutiny more constant, more competent or more alert. None gives its affairs such wide publicity, or tests its financial standing by so frequent balance sheets. Because it has dared to hold itself aloof from all combinations, and been self-reliant enough to manage its own affairs, this outcry has been raised and this warfare begun. How insane are the bellowings, and how treacherous the weapons we have shown. One New York insurance journal even went so far as deliberately to falsify, in its published tabular synopsis of the returns to the New York Insurance Department, the facts in the case of the "Republic." That return, as it appears on the records of the New York Department, is a truthful exhibit of the then condition of the Republic Insurance Co., and shows it in the essential matters of ratio of assets to liabilities, ratio per cent. of premiums received to amount of risk, and soundness and availability of assets, to compare favorably with the best and proudest companies in the land. Such being the case, we think its enemies can hardly afford to continue their attacks, and we know that the "Republic" can afford to await the arbitration of all-testing Time.

PLACES OF AMUSEMENT.

THE OPERA HOUSE.

Crosby's Opera House on Washington, between Dearborn and Clark streets, is one of the chief attractions of the city. As a building, it ranks among the most elegant edifices which adorn the city. As an Opera House, in point of size, beauty of design, and costly architectural decorations, as well as for the perfection of its interior arrangements, it excels any thing of the kind ever established in this country, and almost equals any in Europe. The entire cost of this grand edifice was $450,000. The grand audience room is divided into five separate parts. On the lower floor, first, the orchestra circle, which is entered from the parquette; next, the parquette, which extends nearly to the first tier of galleries; and the parquette circle, embracing the remaining space on either side and fronting the stage. A passage runs around the back of this, and on either side a broad, elegant staircase leads up to the dress circle or first gallery. Last of all, there is the second circle, the front of which is set apart as the family circle. A single tier of three elegant proscenium boxes on each side of the stage, decorated in a most superb and gorgeous style, overlooks the auditorium.

The Opera House has a front of one hundred and forty feet on Washington street, between State and Dearborn, and its depth, from the front to Court place, in the rear, is one hundred and seventy-nine feet. It is four stories high, and is surmounted by a large mansard roof, with elaborate dormer windows. The general style of the structure is decidedly of a modern type of architecture, highly ornate and graceful at first sight, but, like most buildings of the present age, lacking in that massive grandeur, that classic simplicity and repose which best satisfies the imagination. It does not belong to any particular school, but may be characterized as a combination of various styles. If any thing, it has, perhaps, a touch of the Corinthian. The *façade* on Washington street is Athens marble, elaborately cut in tasteful architectural designs. The first or ground floor, is divided into four stores—two on each side of the broad central entrance to the auditorium of the Opera House, which rises from the second story. Three of these are devoted to the sale of music and musical instruments, while the other is occupied by a magnificent restaurant, under the direction of Wright, the Delmonico of Chicago. Here assemble the wealth, beauty and aristocracy of the city. The upper part of the building is divided into a front part, seventy feet in depth; an intermediate passage, seventeen feet wide; and the Opera House proper, which occupies the entire rear portion of the premises, eighty-six feet wide, one hundred and fifty feet in length, and sixty feet high from the parquette floor to the ceiling. The front part of the building on Washington street contains a number of offices and studios; the latter of which are occupied by several of the most distinguished artists in the city. For their convenience there is also arranged on the same floor a spacious picture gallery, lighted from the roof, twenty-eight feet long by fifty-six feet wide, and eighteen feet in height, where at all times may be viewed a choice collection of paintings by the most eminent of foreign and home artists.

Chicago owes this stately pleasure house to the public-spirited liberality and enterprise of Mr. U. H. Crosby, who sacrificed a princely fortune in its erection. The building was completed in the spring of 1865, and the inauguration season of opera commenced on the night of Thursday, May 20, of the same year, when the Opera House, opened for the first time to the public,

McVICKER'S THEATRE.

was filled by one of the most brilliant and fashionable audiences ever assembled on the continent.

It is now under the management of C. D. Hess, and is one of our most popular and elegant places of amusement.

McVICKER'S THEATRE

Is one of the finest structures of the kind in the country. It is situated on Madison street, between State and Dearborn streets. Its cost was over $75,000; and will accommodate about 2,000 people. The exterior, of which an engraving is presented on another page, presents a handsome front on Madison street. The interior arrangements are most complete and admirable The seats are handsomely furnished, easy, and comfortable, affording an excellent view of the stage from all parts of the house. The stage is of an immense size, allowing the production of the spectacular drama on a scale of magnitude and magnficence that can no where be excelled. The dramatic entertainments at this theatre are always of a high order of merit. Strangers can always secure reserved seats at the office of any of the principal hotels.

COL. WOOD'S MUSEUM

Is on Randolph street, between Clark and Dearborn streets. It is a handsome marble front, four-story building. It is divided into several large halls, on the second, third, and fourth floors, which are entered by a spacious stair-case, ascending directly from the street. The museum is filled with an immense number of curiosities of every description; galleries containing paintings, statuary, and works of art; an extensive ornithological collection—one of the most valuable in the United States; a cabinet of minerals and shells; besides numerous other objects of interest and wonder. The specimens of birds and quadrupeds, in the department of natural history, for variety, beauty, and faithfulness to nature, challenge comparison with any other in the world.

In connection with the Museum is the lecture room, where dramatic performances every night, and matinees in the afternoon, are given by an excellent stock company. These performances are most enjoyable and entertaining.

AIKEN'S DEARBORN THEATRE.

This theatre was built in the latter part of 1868, by Mr. D. R. Brant, on the lots Nos. 111 and 113 Dearborn street. It presents a handsome front, fifty feet wide; is one hundred and fifty feet deep, and four stories high. The auditorium commences twenty feet back from the street, is divided into parquette, dress and second circles, and will comfortably accommodate fifteen hundred persons. The seats are models of ease and comfort, being similar to the new style first introduced into Booth's great theatre in New York. This theater was opened in December last by a company from the East, who were not successful in their management. In January last Mr. Frank E. Aiken became lessee; and under his able and experienced direction it has become deservedly popular, and ranks as one of the most entertaining and successful, as it is one of the most beautiful places of amusement in the United States.

THE GERMAN THEATRE,

On N. Wells street, corner of Indiana, is a favorite resort for the sons of Fatherland, the performances being given in German.

TURNER HALL (North Side),

On North Clark street, near Chicago avenue, is a favorite place of amusement. Orchestral entertainments of a high order of excellence are given regularly on Sunday evenings.

TURNER HALL (West Side),

On West Twelfth street, near Halsted, is a popular place of entertainment for the Germans in the West Division.

POLICE, FIRE AND HEALTH DEPARTMENTS.

These three important departments of the city government are vested in a board of commissioners called the Board of Fire and Police Commissioners, who are *ex-officio* a Board of Health. Their offices are on Madison between Clark and La Salle streets.

THE FIRE DEPARTMENT.

Chicago possesses one of the most effective fire departments in the world. It is an exclusively paid department, composed of men who are required to pass through a most rigid examination, as to health, robustness, and temperate habits before they can be admitted members of the force.

FIRE AND POLICE TELEGRAPH.

An important and valuable adjunct of the Fire and Police Departments, is the Fire and Police Telegraph, erected in 1864. Wires from all parts of the city, in every ward, and in almost every block, connect with the main office in the dome of the Court House. By a single turn of the crank in one of the boxes, conspicuously located on nearly every corner in the city, the intelligence of fire, at or near that particular box, or station, is instantly communicated to the office in the Court House dome, from whence the alarm is sounded by electric apparatus in every engine house in the city. Simultaneously, the number of the station is struck by the large bell in the Court House tower, so that the same instant that a fire is discovered, the intelligence of its outbreak and location is communicated to the most remote parts of the city. In the same manner the police are informed of a riot, accident, or any other exigency requiring their attention, or the concentration of their available force.

MASONIC GUIDE.

CITY LODGES.

Lodges.	No.	Meetings.	Halls.
Oriental	33	Friday	Oriental.
Garden City	141	Wednesday	"
Wabansia	160	Monday	"
Germania	182	1st and 3rd Thursdays	Masonic Temple.
Wm. B. Warren	209	2nd and 4th Saturdays	Oriental.
Cleveland	211	1st and 3rd Thursdays	82 W. Randolph st.
Blaney	271	Wednesday	Blaney Hall.
Accordia	277	2nd and 4th Fridays	Lake, S. E. c. Clark.
Ashlar	308	Tuesday	Blair Hall.
Dearborn	310	2nd and 4th Fridays	McVicker's Theatre.
Kilwinning	311	1st and 3rd Thursdays	N. Dearborn, near Kinzie.
Blair	393	Thursday	McVicker's Theatre.
Thos. J. Turner	409	"	Blaney Hall.
Myrethra	410	1st and 3rd Mondays	N. Wells, c. Indiana.
Hesperia	411	Wednesday	Cleveland Lodge.
Hyde Park	422	1st and 3rd Saturdays	Cleaver's Hall.
Chicago	437	1st and 3rd Tuesdays	Oriental Building.
H. W. Bigelow	438	Monday	Masonic Temple.
Home	503	Friday	Cottage Grove, cor. 23rd st.
Pleaides	478	Thursday	147 W. 12th st.
Covenant	526	1st and 3rd Fridays	55 N. Clark st.

Masonic Temple, 83 and 85 Dearborn street; Oriental building, 122 LaSalle street; Blaney Hall, 53 Dearborn street, Blair Hall, over McVicker's Theatre.

ODD-FELLOWS DIRECTORY.

Union Lodge, 48 Clark street, Thursday.
Duane, 48 Clark street, Tuesday.
Excelsior, Washington st., S.E. cor. Dearborn, Wednesday.
Chicago, 48 Clark street, Monday.
Robert Blum (German), 114 Randolph st., Tuesday.
Fort Dearborn, 80 W. Randolph street, Tuesday.
Harmonia, Clinton st., N.E: cor. W. Randolph.
Goethe, 334 Milwaukee av., Thursday.
Hoffnung, S. Canal, nr Mitchell, Wednesday.
North Chicago, N. Wells, cor. Indiana st., Thursday.
Chicago Encampment No. 10, 48 Clark street, 1st and 3rd Friday.
Germania Encampment No. 40 (German), 114 Randolph st., 2nd and 4th Fridays.

130   *Railroad Depots.*

MICHIGAN SOUTHERN R. R. DEPOT.

RAILROAD DEPOTS.

The MICHIGAN SOUTHERN, and CHICAGO, ROCK ISLAND AND PACIFIC trains start from the same depot on Van Buren, opposite LaSalle street.

CHICAGO AND NORTHWESTERN RAILWAY, Galena Division. Depot is on North Wells, corner of North Water street.

ILLINOIS CENTRAL, MICHIGAN CENTRAL, and CHICAGO, BURLINGTON AND QUINCY trains all leave from the Central Illinois depot at the foot of Lake street.

PITTSBURG, FORT WAYNE AND CHICAGO, and CHICAGO, ALTON AND ST. LOUIS trains leave the Union depot, Canal street, opposite West Monroe street.

COLUMBUS, CHICAGO AND INDIANA CENTRAL RAILROAD. THE CHICAGO and MILWAUKEE trains leave from the depot, North Canal street, corner West Kinzie street.

CHICAGO THEATRES.

Crosby's Opera House........Washington, near State.
Dearborn Theatre.............111 and 113 Dearborn.
German Summer Theatre..263 N. Clark, cor. Chestnut.
German Theatre..............N. Wells, cor. Indiana.
McVicker's Theatre...Madison, bet. State & Dearborn.
Turner Hall......cor. Milwaukee ave., near Carpenter.
Turner Hall..............cor. N. Clark and Chestnut.
Turner Hall................W. Twelfth, near Halsted.
Wood's Museum...Randolph. bet. Clark and Dearborn.

CITY RAILWAY AND OMNIBUS ROUTES.

Cars leave corner of State and Randolph streets every few minutes *via* State street to Cottage Grove, Indiana avenue, and Southern city limits. Also, by

State street and Archer avenue to Bridgeport, and during this summer will be extended to Brighton.

Cars also leave same place every few minutes *via* Madison street to Western city limits, and *via* Madison and Halsted streets, southwestwardly, along Blue Island avenue to Mitchel street.

Cars also leave same place every few minutes *via* Randolph street to Union Park and Western city limits, and *via* Halsted street, northwestwardly, along Milwaukee avenue to city limits.

North Chicago Horse Railway Cars, leave Lake street for city limits, every 13 minutes; for Sedgwick street, every 13 minutes; for Clybourn avenue and Larrabee street, every 13 minutes; for Graceland, without change of car, every hour and 50 minutes. Cars leave city limits for Lake street every 13 minutes; leave corner Larrabee and Centre for same, every 13 minutes; leave corner North avenue and Sedgwick street for same, every 39 minutes; leave Graceland for Lake street every hour.

OMNIBUSES.

Run to and from all the principal hotels and railroad depots on the arrival and departure of all trains. A line of omnibuses has also been recently started from Lake street *via* Madison and Halsted streets, to the lumber region in the southwest division of the city; another line runs along Wabash avenue to the city limits, and another from same street, along Milwaukee avenue, to northwestern city limits.

HACKS AND CARRIAGES.

The Hack stand is on Court House Square. Hackmen are not allowed to charge any more than the following rates. When they charge more than these rates, they can not collect any thing for their services:

For conveying each passenger from one railroad depot to another railroad depot, fifty cents; for conveying each passenger not exceeding one mile, fifty cents; for conveying a passenger any distance over one mile, and not less than two miles, one dollar; for each

Hacks and Carriages.

additional passenger, of the same party or family, fifty cents; for conveying a passenger in said city any distance exceeding two miles, one dollar and fifty cents; for each additional passenger of the same family or party, fifty cents; for conveying children between five and fourteen years of age, half of the above prices may be charged for like distances; but for children under five years of age no charge shall be made; *Provided*, that the distance from any railroad depot, steamboat landing or hotel, to any other railroad depot, steamboat landing or hotel, shall, in all cases, be estimated as not exceeding one mile; for the use, by the day, of any hackney coach or other vehicle, drawn by two horses, or other animals, with one or more passengers, eight dollars per day; for the use of any such carriage or vehicle by the hour, with one or more passengers, with the privilege of going from place to place, and stopping as often as may be required, as follows: for the first hour, two dollars; for each additional hour, or part of an hour, one dollar; for conveying one or more passengers to or from any place in said city, between the hours of twelve o'clock, midnight, and seven o'clock A. M., for each trip, without regard to distance, or number of passengers, two dollars; for the use of any cab or vehicle drawn by one horse, or other animal, by the hour, with the privilege of going from place to place, with one or more passengers, and stopping when required: for the first hour, one dollar; for each additional hour, or part of an hour, fifty cents; for the use of any such carriage, by the day, four dollars. Every passenger shall be allowed to have conveyed on such vehicle, without charge, his ordinary traveling baggage, not exceeding, in any case, one trunk and twenty-five pounds of other baggage. For every additional package, when the whole weight of baggage is over one hundred pounds, if conveyed to any place within the city limits, the owner or driver may be permitted to charge fifteen cents.

CEMETERIES.

The principal Cemeteries, for beauty of decoration and extent of ground, are Graceland, Calvary and Rose Hill. The following is the location of all the Cemeteries belonging to Chicago, with their offices, where visitors must procure tickets of admission:

GRACELAND — Two miles north of the city, on Green Bay road. Office, 89 Clark street.

ROSE HILL — Seven miles north of the city, on the Milwaukee railway. Office, 151 Lake street.

CALVARY — (Catholic) — Ten miles north of the city, on the Milwaukee railway. Office, 15 Madison street.

GERMAN CATHOLIC — Three miles from city limits, on Green Bay road.

GERMAN LUTHERAN — South of Graceland.

CITY — On Green Bay road. Office, 2 Court House. There are four Hebrew Cemeteries, all on Green Bay road, from one to two miles north of city limits.

OAKWOOD — On the Illinois Central railroad, eight miles from the city. Office, 33 LaSalle street.

CHICAGO HOTELS.

Adams House,..............Lake, cor. Michigan Ave.
Briggs House,..................Randolph, cor. Wells.
Central House..................180 and 182 Randolph.
City Hotel......................Lake, S. E. cor. State.
Everett House.............cor. Clark and Van Buren.
Garden City House..........cor. Madison and Market.
Hough House....................Union Stock Yards.
Laclede Hotel ....W. Madison, cor. Canal.
Massasoit House...........S. Water, cor. Central Ave.
Matteson House.......Dearborn, N. W. cor. Randolph.
Metropolitan Hotel........Randolph, S. W. cor Wells.
Oldridge House................State, cor. Van Buren.
Orient House..................State, cor. Van Buren.
Revere House......................Clark, cor. Kinzie.
Richmond House.........S. Water, cor. Michigan Ave.
Sherman House..........Clark, N. W. cor. Randolph.

St. Cloud........................112 and 114 Franklin.
St. James...................cor. Washington and State.
Tremont House.............Dearborn, S. E. cor. Lake.
Washington House.............244 and 246 Randolph.

TREMONT HOUSE.

The visitor to Chicago can not fail to be attracted by the splendid and massive structure of the Tremont House, which is centrally located on the corner of Dearborn and Lake streets. This hotel is widely known as one of the most spacious and agreeable in the West. The internal arrangements admirably harmonize with the inviting aspect of the exterior. The Tremont was rebuilt, remodeled, and refurnished in the richest and most luxurious style in 1868. It comprises nearly three hundred rooms—single and in suites—with baths, closets, and every modern improvement attached. The reading rooms, smoking rooms, public and private parlors, billiard rooms, saloons, etc,, are all on the most comfortable and elegant scale—no expense having been spared in their fitting up. The ladies' parlors are furnished at an expense of $10,000. Atwood's celebrated improved passenger elevator has been introduced, for the conveyance of guests to the different floors, saving them the time and trouble of climbing numerous flights of stairs. The table is richly provided, and the *cuisine* unsurpassed in bounty and elegance. The employes of the house are noted for their obliging and courteous demeanor, and no guest can possibly be subjected to rudeness or inattention.

The Tremont is situated in the very heart of the great business thoroughfares, and is within easy reach of all the theatres, places of public resort, and railroad depots. Combining all the qualities of a first class house, it offers superior inducements to all who visit the Garden City on business or for pleasure. In the past the Tremont has deservedly enjoyed an enviable reputation, but, at the present time, it is, if possible, more faultlessly conducted than ever, it being the laudable ambition of the urbane and generous proprietor, John B. Drake, Esq., to render his

TREMONT HOUSE.

BRIGGS HOUSE.

hotel the very *beau ideal* of comfort and convenience, combining all the freedom of public, with the contentment of home life. Among the many popular traits of the Tremont, its special parlors are always at the command of the citizens of Chicago, for the meetings of committees, on all matters interesting to the public. In all its relations this popular hotel is attractive and hospitable, and well deserves the patronage which it has so long and so extensively enjoyed.

BRIGGS HOUSE.

This first-class hotel is justly celebrated among the traveling public. Its location is central, on the northeast corner of Randolph and Wells street. It is near the Chamber of Commerce and the Court House, and therefore convenient of access to the business portion of the city, places of amusement, etc. It has been recently thoroughly renovated and refurnished with new and elegant furniture, and fitted, from basement to attic, with all the modern appointments and appliances of a first class hotel, Every possible convenience is provided for the weary traveler that good taste, abundant means and many years' experience in the business can suggest or supply. The dining hall is spacious, elegant, well ventilated, and attended by polite and attentive waiters under the supervision of "mine host" and accomplished steward. The table is bountifully supplied with the delicacies, dainties, and substantials which the market can supply, and a *cuisine* unsurpassed for its excellence can prepare.

RESTAURANTS.

Chicago is well supplied with admirably managed restaurants, among the more prominent and popular of which is that of Messrs. Collins & McGuire, which is described by the *Chicago Times*, May 23rd, 1869, as follows:

Restaurants.

Among the most noticeable evidences of the fact that Chicago is rapidly following in the footsteps of New York is the establishment of an elegant and expensively fitted up fancy grocery store and merchants' lunch room, at No. 119 Dearborn street, by Messrs. Collins & McGuire, two gentlemen well known in Chicago as business men of the first class. The front of the store is handsomely fitted up with a solid walnut counter and tastefully arranged shelving. This part of the establishment is devoted to the branch of excellent brands of cigars and tobacco, with some of the finest pipes in Chicago upon the one side, and a large stock of all varieties of French and other fancy groceries on the other. Upon the counter stands a fine glass show-case, while suspended from the ceiling hangs a magnificent bronze chandelier, imported especially by Mr. Henry Byrne, of this city.

Passing through a fine series of folding doors, composed of walnut frames, filled in with green "rep," and surmounted by a gilt eagle, the merchants' lunch and sample room is reached. Upon either side of the doors a fine arch is further ornamented by an elaborate cage, containing a beautiful canary bird. Under the right hand arch is the office of the firm, a cozy little place, with a richly carved walnut desk.

The floor of the front store is of black and white marble, while that of the lunch room is of black walnut and ash, placed in diamond form. Both ceilings are covered with the richest and handsomest French paper, embellished by suitable designs and a profusion of gilt moulding.

In the lunch-room the most prominent feature is a massively carved walnut bar, behind which, laid in the deep walnut paneling of the most elaborate design, is a gigantic mirror 13 feet 4 inches in length, 6 feet 10 inches in height, and valued at $1,000. Over the mirror, in niches in the carved paneling, are busts of Henry Clay and Daniel Webster, one upon either side. At the end of the bar is a heavy walnut ale and wine box, surmounted in the centre by a gilt framed time piece. Upon one side of the box rests a bust of Abraham Lincoln, carved in walnut; upon the other a small bust of Stephen A. Douglas; while over the two is placed George Washington. The walls are covered with rich French paper, arranged in gilt-framed panels, and presenting some gems of Continental scenery. The ornamentation of the room is further increased by two beautiful pictures, one represeting "Winter," and the other "Summer," placed in niches in the walnut, on either side of the bar.

Leading from the lunch-room is a conveniently arranged lavatory and other necessary offices.

On descending the stairs which lead to the basement, the visitor is first ushered into a cozy wine room, furnished in handsome style. The floor is covered by an expensive Brussels carpet, while the walls and ceiling are ornamented by costly French paper of rich design. Upon this same floor, and to the rear, is the stock and bottling room, a large and cool apartment, filled to the ceiling with the choicest ales, wines, and all varieties of liquors. Here Messrs. Collins & McGuire have every facility for bottling any quantity of the various varieties of liquors, which they are prepared to dispose of in lots to suit families, at the most satisfactory terms.

Leading from the stock room is the kitchen, fitted up with a fine range, of itself calculated to make the lunch room a perfect success. This room is connected with the restaurant above by an elevator of the most approved construction.

Messrs. Collins & McGuire, the enterprising proprietors of this establishment, are both well known in this city. Mr. William Collins has been, for nearly five years, engaged in business of this nature, and formerly was connected with the Tremont House. Mr. McGuire, until last fall, when he associated himself with Mr. Collins, was in the provision line upon the West side, and previous to that was prominently known in commercial circles in Niagara, Canada.

The carpenter work upon this fine establishment was all executed by Cochran & Mullins, carpenters and builders, No. 271 Superior street. It is of a most excellent character, and speaks in the highest terms of the ability of the carpenters. This branch of the fitting up

Restaurants.

embraces some of the finest pieces of carving and moulding in walnut ever seen in the West.

The painting was the work of Mr. McDermott, recently of Philadelphia, and is also of the finest character. Mr. McDermott is the man who recently executed the painting at the Western News Company, on State street, and in both instances he has shown powers of workmanship of the highest order.

The papering was all laid on by J. J. McGrath; the mirror was imported by Noble, and the entire improvement effected under the architectural supervision of John R. Winchell. The upholstering was done by Hollister & Phelps, and the furniture is from the establishment of F. Porter Thayer & Co.

A branch of the establishment is on the northwest corner of Clark and South Water streets, which is in every respect a complete lunch-room for merchants.

THE NEATEST and most complete first-class Oyster and Ice Cream Saloon in the city, is that lately opened by Messrs. Smith & Odlin. The former is known as the "Chicago Oyster King," and the latter as the "Champion Confectioner." This establishment, located at No. 79 Clark street, is fitted up exquisitely and with every modern improvement, and supplies a want which strangers and citizens always experience in visiting a large city, namely: a first-class Ladies' Oyster and Ice Cream Saloon. In this establishment all the luxuries and delicacies of the season will be served up in the best style: a good stew, a nice fry, or "on the shell," will always be found at this establishment. When in season, can always be had here, in every variety, shell crabs, scallops, smelts, eastern speckled trout, frogs, lobsters, shrimps, clams, etc., and such a variety of shell oysters as can not be surpassed in any other establishment in Chicago. The Ice Cream department will be found complete in every particular. It is important for strangers visiting Chicago, to know where a delicious ice cream, soda water, a mint julep, a milk punch, choicest brands of imported champagnes and other wines, and all other cooling beverages can be had, together with an endless assortment of the purest and most delicious confectionery. Strangers, tourists, and parties visiting Chicago would do well to keep this establishment in view. It is one of the most complete of the kind to be found any where. Accommodating and attentive waiters will be found always on hand. A Restaurant is connected with this establishment, where a nice steak, a veal cutlet, a mutton chop, etc., with every luxury can always be had.

THE STATE MICROSCOPICAL SOCIETY OF ILLINOIS.

This society was organized in the winter of 1868, and was incorporated by the legislature, under its present name, during the session of 1869. It already possesses many valuable instruments, with suitable and costly apparatus. It numbers among its members, not only the leading members of the learned professions, but also many of those whose lives have been spent in accumulating fortunes by trade and commerce, whose noble pride it is to contribute in making Chicago what she is fast becoming—a great centre for the cultivation of the arts and sciences.

ART GALLERIES.

Art in Chicago is still in its infancy. Prior to 1860 it had hardly obtained a foothold here. A few of our wealthy citizens had adorned their residences with fine pictures, which they brought home from their European tours; but there was no public spirit in art matters. There were no studios, no schools of art or design, no galleries of pictures, no places of resort for the artists or connoisseurs, and no inducement for artists to settle here.

The first impulse which was given to art in a public

direction was the distribution of the Chicago Art Union at Hesler's photograph gallery, which took place December 7th, 1860.

The result of this exhibition was manifest in the collection of works exhibited in 1863, in McVicker's Theatre building, for the benefit of the Northwestern Sanitary Fair, which was opened October 27th.

In 1864 William Beebe, a connoisseur and dealer in pictures, brought a very meritorious collection of copies of old masters and some works of the modern European painters to this city.

The progress of art was now so rapid that art galleries were established in various business houses, prominent among which, that of Matson & Co. enjoys an excellent reputation. Hovey & Heffron also originated one of the finest galleries, which is still in existence, and filled with the choicest of works. In addition to this gallery, the Opera House Art Gallery, under the supervision of Mr. Aitken, and Jevne & Almini's gallery, under the supervision of Mr. Frodsham, are now in successful operation, and are constantly full of fine American and foreign pictures.

ACADEMY OF DESIGN.

Mr. Volk, President of the Academy of Design, who was commissioned to make a collection of casts, while abroad, for the use of the students, at an expense of $5000, has furnished the appended list of about fifty of the seventy pieces.'

The casts will be placed upon exhibition so soon as the Academy gets settled in new quarters, which will be in a building of their own.

The Fighting Gladiator; Bust of the Farnese Hercules; Bust of Young Augustus; Genius of the Vatican; Basso-Relievo from the Parthenon; Bust of Homer; Bust of the Apollo Belvidere; Horse's Head (from the bronze); Bust of the Cupid of the Vatican; Bust of the Faun of the Vatican; Bust of the Apollo and Muses; Torso of Theseus (copy), from the Parthenon; Bust of Minerva; Boy and Thorn (from a bronze statue); Three Hands and a Foot; Feet from Canova's

Gladiator; Feet from the Farnese Hercules and Antinous; Feet from a Colossal Antique; Bust of Ariadne; Boy and Goose; Anatomical Head, from Nature; Flamming's Cupid; Head and Body of the Venus di Milo; Anatomical Torso, from Nature; Anatomical Leg and Arms; Torso of Theseus, from the Parthenon; Anatomical Figure; Bust of Psyche of Naples; Flora of the Capitol; Bust of Venus; Bassi-Relievi, by Benvenuto Cellini; Two Children's Heads, by Flamming; Torso of the Apollo Belvidere; Bust of Niobe; Back of Female, from Nature; Bust of Ajax; The Dioscobolus, or Quoit-Thrower; Female Antique Face; Head and Face of Constantine; Casts from Trojan's Column; Colossal Arm (from a bronze in the Vatican); Basso-Relievo, Faun and Tiger; Cuirass of Augustus, from the Vatican; Five Bassi-Relievi, from the Parthenon; five from the Temple of Victory, and a Torso from the same.

SCULPTURE.

The sculptor's art is well represented in Chicago. Mr. L. W. Volk has made a name among connoiseurs in art matters, by his statue of Douglas and bust of Lincoln, and in this country his name has become celebrated for his many equally excellent works. Amongst the latter we may name the Soldiers' Monument, recently erected in the city of Rock Island, and the Firemen's Monument, at Rose Hill, which have been pronounced, by competent judges, in true artistic design and accuracy of execution unsurpassed by anything of the kind in this city. In the studio of this distinguished artist can now be seen the design for a Cook County soldiers' monument, to be erected in Rose Hill Cemetery, to cost about $20,000. The monument will be about 40 feet high, of granite, including the figure of a soldier, to be of pure Italian marble or bronze. It will be decorated with elaborate and appropriate relief. The design was selected by the committee from twenty-one competitors, embracing some of the ablest sculptors in the country. The Chicago Marble and Granite Works Manufacturing Company, who have the execution of the monument in charge, is located on Washington, near Franklin street. In their extensive warerooms can be seen, at all times, many most elaborate and beautiful designs for monuments, tombs, and mantels, displaying a high degree of finish and excellence. This company import their marble direct from Italy, and granite from Scotland and the New England States.

Mr Volk has recently returned from an extended tour through the art galleries in Europe. He has established a studio in Rome, Italy, where he proposes spending a part of his time for a few years, in the personal supervision of such works as he may execute there.

MUSEUM OF ART AND HORTICULTURE.

The establishment of Messrs. Hovey & Heffron, No. 87 State street, presents a center of attraction to those who desire to make home, within and without, a paradise. Here may be seen a multitude of articles, combining the works of God and man, for the beautifying of house and garden. It is not now necessary or needful for those who wish to secure the beauties of nature in fruit or flower, or choice works in paintings, sculpture, or carvings, to travel beyond Chicago for them. As well, if not better, than at New York, Philadelphia, or Boston, can be purchased here—the masterpieces of American artists; the creations of European genius, and the beautiful handiworks of Deity. It is the aim, and has been the achievement of this house to meet the wants and tastes of an intelligent community with articles for sale good in quality, unexcelled in taste, and as economical in price as any European or American market can furnish. In their gallery of art can always be found the very best works of native and foreign artists, in oil paintings, marble, water colors, and every form of Aquarelle. Their French water color *fac-similes* are copies of the best *genre* pictures of the French school, from subjects in the Academy, Louvre, etc., giving perfect copies of the works of the best Paris artists at a nominal sum, thus bringing the gems of Meissonier, Carbonel, Gérome, etc., within the reach of many. (The least costly originals of these are held at $1,000 each.) In Sepia, India ink, pencil, and other drawings and designs they offer a very large variety, on all sorts of materials, but especially adapted for center table and toilet use.

Passing from the gallery into the ware-room various articles of bronze invite examination. Along the sides of this apartment an endless variety of articles in Parian are seen; here also are exhibited, from their Terra Cotta works, many varied forms of ornamental art, particularly in architectural work. In its susceptibility for ornament, indestructibility, and very moderate cost, Terra Cotta, as a building material, in this section and climate, has proved itself especially adapted. The delicate and tasteful ornaments known as alabaster, cut and chiseled by hand, from the soft Carrara marble, are here in profusion; also a large and rich class of goods made in rare woods—lemon, sandal, olive, cedar, etc., plain and richly inlaid, of many colors and designs, which are known to travelers and connoiseurs as Sorrento work. Of Chinese and Japanese wares they keep a full supply. By a new process—the invention of a French artist, now in the employ of this firm—they are enabled to furnish vases and baskets of fruit, a perfect counterfeit of nature, in size, weight, form, texture, and color, and also susceptible of being handled and cleaned when soiled. They will furnish specimens of extraordinary sized prize fruits and vegetables, preserved by this system, and duplicated, upon receipt of samples, at trifling cost.

Their horticultural department is equal to any in the country. Citizens and strangers are cordially invited, by the courteous proprietors, to visit their establishment. Parties can rely upon this house as offering only the best wares. The honor, as well as the taste, of the gentlemen comprising this firm is highly appreciated by the citizens of Chicago, and their establishment is the pride of the city.

ARCHITECTURE.—Chicago having now reached an assured position as a great metropolis of commerce, manufactures, and influence, she can afford to devote much of her energy and wealth to the growth and culture of æsthetic taste in her midst, and in her public and private buildings, their adornments and surroundings, to illustrate the taste for the beautiful and true in nature and art, which in all enlightened communities, when prosperous, finds development and patronage. In the cultivation of this taste much depends upon the abilities of the architect who fashions the public buildings. In this respect Chicago has been, in one instance, at least, particularly fortunate, and our citizens refer with pride to one of the oldest architects in the city, Mr. W. W. Boyington, when pointing out to strangers some of our noblest public structures, the creations of his genius, not the least of which is the First Baptist Church, a representation of which is presented on page 87 of this book.

O'BRIEN'S ART EMPORIUM.—There is no city in the United States which, to-day, in proportion to its age and population, can boast of so large a number, such hard-working, and such talented artists as the city of Chicago. It is also true, that in no city are there greater facilities, both as to quality and price, for the purchase of the numerous varieties of art which contribute to the pleasure and contentment of society. We have been convinced of this by an extended visit to O'Brien's art emporium, at No. 51 State street, where we have always been received cordially, and permitted to revel at will among the exhaustless resources that it affords. Two observations have been especially prominent:

First. The ample room obtained in the new location, the enterprise that is characteristic of Chicago, and the experience and excellent judgment employed, have rendered this a depository of art which can not be surpassed on the continent. It is no longer necessary that our citizens should go to London, Paris, or New York to purchase any thing that appertains to the ar s, whether it be painting in oil or water colors; framing, of the latest and most elegant descriptions; engravings, modern or ancient, rare old line or artists' proofs; chromo-lithographs, the great popularizers of art, of every nation, school, and style; photographs, in the

O'BRIEN'S ART EMPORIUM,
51 STATE ST., CHICAGO.

highest finish of the art and in the largest variety; materials for artists, aids to students, ornaments for home, or what not—we find that, at last, all these may be obtained in Chicago as surely and to better advantage than by sending or going to other cities for them.

Second. We find the resources for ornamentation and the beautifying of homes so great and varied; extending in character and price to all tastes and to all conditions of people; offering such irresistible charms as we ourselves never dreamed of. Any one who will take the pleasure—it is no trouble—to examine the assortment at the Art Emporium will find that there is no occasion for going outside of it, or looking to other sources, for a supply of art matters in all forms and at all prices.

"Art is truth, and art is religion, and its study and practice a daily work of pious duty," says Thackeray. But it has other and yet more attractive charms than this moral view possesses. Art appeals at once to the mind and the heart, to the intellect and to the affections. Every good picture has a good story to tell; a variety of good pictures presents a variety of sensations and reflections, which form a constant and never failing source of enjoyment. Who has not been made cheerful by the contemplation of a bright and happy scene? Who has a good picture in his house that does not recur to it again and again, with renewed interest and enjoyment, and is not better and more contented for such contemplation? And modern art, with its improvements, has brought within the means of nearly every one the possession, not of pictures alone, but of a collection of pictures—all good and enjoyable. Show us the pictures that decorate a wall, and we will tell you of the tastes, the happiness, and the pleasures of the dwellers. If any one who reads this feels the necessity of demonstration to be convinced of the truth of it, let him visit Mr. O'Brien's Art Emporium, and we venture to say, that he will not come away under a couple of hours, and when he does he will willingly admit all that we have said.

And there can be no doubt in the mind of any reasonable person, that, in every sense of the word, it pays to invest in pictures. Once convinced in this view of the matter, the practical people of the country will make the investment more largely than ever. It pays in the comfort and enjoyment which pictures bring. It pays in the advancement of taste and enlargement of culture. It pays in the satisfaction found in affording friends the hospitality of an elegant or cheerful home. And the humble home which is rich in its possession of bright and happy pictures, is more elegant to a refined person than the gaudy home that abounds in elegant and meretricious display. There is one picture—"Purity"—which is all that its name suggests—pure in conception, in design, in execution, and delicately and artistically beautiful, which is worth more in its influence than thousands of dollars.

In the Art Emporium will be found a greater number and a wider selection of rare old line engravings than has ever before been exhibited in the West, and as complete and valuable a collection as has ever been made in America. The engravings of this collection represent every school, every nation, every age, and every prominent artist that the world has produced. The scope of subjects is almost illimitable, and includes a variety that can not fail to please the taste of every one who may desire to select.

Among the chromos are those of the English, American, French, German, and Italian schools. English chromos are seldom printed to produce an oil effect. They are intended to represent water-color paintings; and they are generally superior to their European rivals. There is a delicacy in their finish and tone that neither the Germans nor Italians attain. Yet all have their distinguishing merits. Teachers, decorate your schools. Pictures have an historical value, a refining influence, and a cheerful quality, which can not but be most beneficial to forming minds. Something appropriate will always be found at the Art Emporium.

Besides the paintings, engravings, and chromos that have been mentioned, there are beautiful and artistic lithographs; photographs; stereoscopic views; oil prints; enamel paintings; beautiful ornaments in

Parian and Iceland Spar; drawing studies; church pictures; a variety of illuminations in Decalcomanie and Diaphonie; a varied and full collection of artists' materials. Particular attention is given to framing. It is not necessary that the frame should always be expensive, but it *is* necessary that it should be in good taste and thoroughly adapted to the picture for which it is intended. It is essential that there should always be an immense and varied stock, such as is constantly kept at the Art Emporium, from which to make selection. It is also advisable that the purchaser should listen to the advice of some practical and experienced framer, and it would be well to consult with Mr. O'BRIEN, who manufactures largely in all styles and varieties, and has done so for years.

Finally, let us impress upon the reader, that he will always be welcome to O'Brien's Art Emporium, 51 State street, as a visitor, whether he desires to purchase or not; and that, as a visitor, he will find an enjoyment that will fully repay him for the trouble he may take, in the enjoyment which it affords.

READER OF THE GUIDE, if you desire to pass an hour pleasantly, as well as profitably, or if contemplating purchasing articles to beautify your home, or offer to your customers, for like purpose, do not forget the *Repository of Fine Art*, of Messrs. McIntyre, Peck & Co., 136 State Street. This extensive and model establishment ranks foremost in this branch of Chicago enterprise. Their spacious and tastefully arranged store is filled with an immense stock of every thing that pertains to Art. Their Retail Department displays for exhibition, and sale — richly framed — Paintings from the easels of celebrated home and foreign artists; Water Colors; American, French, German, and the finest Italian Chromos. A choice selection of Engravings adorn the walls, which includes Artist's Proofs and India Prints, Lithograghs, Photographs, etc., etc. Swiss carved goods, and other ornamental wares, fill their beautiful show cases — in fact, all that can please the eye, and satisfy the most fastidious taste, is to be found in their stock. They have also, for the lover of Billiards, Briggs' new Patent Parlor Billiard Table — ready with balls and cue for a trial of its merits. They are exclusive agents for the Northwest for this desirable article of home adornment and pleasure.

The Wholesale Department comprises a full stock of Pictures, and picture requisites, for the trade, Frames, Mouldings, Cord, Tassels, etc., etc.

They have exclusive control of a line of specialties that will pay to examine. Buyers should not forget to look in at 136 State Street, and examine goods and prices.

PHOTOGRAPH GALLERIES.

The stranger, in visiting the photograph galleries of Chicago, should take a note of the location of Carbutt's, No. 24 Washington street. His elegant parlors are adorned with specimens of his art, equal to any that can be produced in the profession any where. His Berlin photographs, from retouched negatives, are most exquisite productions of the highest skill, and present all the beauty of porcelain miniatures. At a recent assembly of the State Microscopical Society in this city, Mr. Carbutt both astonished and delighted the critical audience by an exhibition of many beautiful objects photo-micographed by him with the oxy-hydrogen microscope.

THE TINTYPE is comparatively a new feature in Art, having been practiced but a very few years, and the first introduction of this beautiful branch of Photography west of New York, was about eighteen months ago, at 122 Lake Street, Chicago, by Mr. Alfred Hall, an artist of over twenty years experience in the photographic business. Mr. Hall was engaged, for about two years, in other business, but even the activity and excitement of a mercantile life in Chicago could not divert his attention from his old profession, so he made up his mind to start his cherished art again, but by close observation he discovered that the old process of making a negative, and printing on paper, was entirely too slow and expensive for this fast age, consequently

Art Galleries.

he decided to fit up a first class Gallery, with all the appointments completely adapted to this new and beautiful branch of the art, and make it a specialty. While the process of fitting the Gallery was going on, it was remarked by some of the old photographers that Hall must be crazy, to think of making that one style of pictures pay in Chicago, but it is evident they knew not what they were talking about, for in less than two months the Tintype became so popular that he found it necessary to fit up a branch Gallery to accommodate his customers, and at the present time he is setting more people, at 122 Lake Street, than any other two Galleries in the city. The instruments used are constructed especially for this branch of the art, being a cluster of tubes arranged so nicely that, with a properly sensitized plate, from one to three dozen pictures can be produced almost instantaneously, consequently it is one of the most sure methods of getting children's pictures known. Every stranger visiting Chicago should be sure to go to Hall's, at 122 Lake Street, as it is the original and only exclusive Tintype Gallery in the city, and sit for a dozen of those beautiful pictures. It will hinder you only about twenty minutes to get them taken and finished, and will cost but two shillings.

THE CITY OF PARIS,

In miniature, can be seen by the visitor to Chicago at Stein's unique and elegant bazaar, No. 83 South Clark street. The collection of fancy goods, toys, and elegant ornaments he keeps in stock in this beautiful bazaar is wonderful and well worth seeing. It is bewildering to both mind and eye to see the thousand and one useful and ornamental articles you are invited to select from for one dollar. Stein's Bazaar, 83 South Clark street, is one of the institutions of Chicago, and, like many other of her institutions, must be seen before it can be appreciated.

HOME MANUFACTURES.

WHAT THINGS ARE MADE IN CHICAGO.

WHERE THEY ARE MADE AND WHO MAKES THEM.

Occupying the entire north side of Fulton street, between Jefferson and Desplaines streets, with a frontage of 320 feet, and extending to the rear 170 feet, is the planing mill and factory of S. I. Russell. The original of the present establishment was constructed in 1859, and totally destroyed by fire in the following year. Having been rebuilt immediately, it escaped the perils of conflagration until December of last year, when it was again burnt to the ground. Within a month thereafter it was rebuilt for a second time, and put in complete working order.

The ground floor of the factory is devoted to planing and moulding purposes. There are in operation here, among other machinery, six steam planers, capable of dressing 70,000 feet of lumber per day.

On the second floor may be found a room 170 by 90 feet in dimensions, where are made up sashes, doors, and blinds. This is thoroughly equipped with the best approved machinery and other appliances, and we believe cannot be excelled for completeness and adaptation to the purposes for which it is used in the entire Western country.

Adjoining this apartment, on the left, is another, 60 by 50 feet, where the operations of turning, scroll-sawing, and the like are carried on. Five scroll saws and a very ingeniously constructed fluting machine for the doing of various kinds of ornamental and fancy woodwork for balusters, etc., make lively music the whole working day long. Eight men are constantly busy here upon stair-work

Through the center of the building and connecting the various floors, there rises an elevator 7x18 feet, by means of which the material is raised to the different departments, and the finished work sent below for shipment or delivery.

A pair of heavy iron doors open from the west end of this floor into the dry house. This is doubtless the largest and best constructed building of the kind ever erected in this city. It is of dimensions 42x62 feet, and four stories in height. The first story is divided into four kilns. A boiler weighing 12 tons and 10,000 feet of steam pipe are required to generate and distribute the heat. Each floor of the factory is connected with the dry house in the same manner as before described in the case of the second And all the wood-work turned out by the factory is, before being put together, thoroughly dried and seasoned in this department. The upper floors have not yet been fitted up with their appliances, but will be in a few weeks.

On the north-west corner of the ground is located a machine shop, where the planers and other machines in the factory are manufactured. This department is very well and conveniently arranged. A number of skillful mechanics, supplied with all the necessary apparatus, are employed here. Three large forges constitute a portion of the equipment. These are of the latest and best construction, and would delight the soul of old Tubal Cain to look upon, though they would doubtless puzzle that ancient blacksmith somewhat at first. The blasts are supplied to them by machinery. The larger share of all the machines in the factory were made here, and quite a large business is also done in manufacturing wood working machinery, for sale to the trade. This establishment also manufactures the wood-work, planing and matching machines, and railroad chairs for depots, which are made a specialty.

The engine which furnishes motive power for the whole establishment is of 300 horse power, and a model of mechanical workmanship. The engine and boiler rooms are very securely built, with heavy brick arches, and are so protected by strong iron frame work, through which the fuel is passed into the furnaces, as to guard as effectually as possible against communicating fire to, or receiving it from other portions of the establishment.

Nearly opposite the factory, at the corner of Fulton and Desplaines streets, is a large brick building, 80 feet front by 90 feet deep, and five stories in height, where are located the offices, sales-rooms, and store-rooms. The main office is roomy, pleasant, and very neatly furnished. Its walls are protected by a neat wainscoting of pine and black walnut. Private offices, provided with wash and bath rooms, closets, etc., etc., are connected with it, and supply "all the modern conveniences." Anthony S. Goodridge, Esq., an experienced and most courteous gentleman, has charge of affairs here as chief clerk.

Among the immense stock of material in the store-rooms, we noticed one lot of doors which had just been finished up and were then ready for shipment, in fulfillment of an order of $40,000. Besides these there were sashes, doors, blinds, mouldings, brackets, stair-railings, balusters, window-frames, etc., etc., in seeming endless quantities. Seats for churches and railway depots are furnished here in great numbers. Mr. Russell's orders for work of this kind are numerous, and come from all portions of the Northwest. Mr. R. also builds railway passenger and freight houses at his factory; that is to say, he frames and fits them completely, so that, after their arrival on the ground, they need but to be put together. On Tuesday last he shipped three complete passenger houses for the Pittsburg, Fort Wayne and Chicago railroad company, and has several others in course of construction. Carpenters, builders, and contractors can find every thing here in the way of patterns and designs for all the varieties of wood work entering into the construction of buildings.

In connection with the establishment is an extensive factory, where are made the celebrated Churchill's patent splint baskets, of and in which Mr. Russell is the sole manufacturer and dealer. The baskets are of four different styles, known respectively as "grain," "market," "laundry," and "feed." There are six sizes of the first, nine of the second, three of the third, and five of the last.

The splints and ribs, or standards, are made mostly of elm lumber, and are manufactured by a newly patented machine, by which all the materials are planed smooth.

Judging from what we saw of them, there is no basket known to the trade which, for neatness, strength, and durability, as well as for excellence of workmanship, surpasses those made by Mr. Russell. We can see no good reason why our Western dealers should send hundreds of miles to the East for articles in this line, which are inferior in quality, and superior only in the altitude of their prices, when their orders can be supplied here in any quantity, and at the shortest possible notice. We advise our Chicago and other Western woodenware men to investigate this matter, and see whether there is not here a chance for them to secure larger profits for themselves and better satisfaction to their customers.

We conclude this short and imperfect sketch of one of the leading manufacturing establishments—or rather combination of establishments—of Chicago by giving a few figures, which indicate the extent of the business done.

There are employed by Mr. Russell 200 hands, to whom is paid weekly over $2,000. The capital invested in buildings, stock, and machinery is $225,000, and last year's sales amounted to a million of dollars.

FURNITURE.—For over fifteen years past the firm of A. L. Hale & Brother have been engaged in business in this city, as manufacturers and importers of, and dealers in, Furniture. The gentlemen composing the firm are well known, active and enterprising men, who, by steadfast devotion and untiring effort, have built up a very large and lucrative trade, so that they now take rank among the principal Furniture dealers of Chicago and the Northwest.

They now occupy the whole of the large building numbered 10, 12, 14 and 16 on North Canal street, with their Factory and Warerooms. The structure is five stories in height, and has a frontage of 80 feet, with a rear extension of 160 feet. They formerly used but a

FIELD, LEITER & CO'S ESTABLISHMENT.

portion of the building, but have recently been compelled by the increase of their business to take more room.

The various floors up to the fifth, exclusive of the space occupied for office purposes, are filled with an immense stock, embracing all the varieties known to the trade, from the cheapest and plainest, suited to furnish the humble cabin of the pioneer to the most luxurious and costly for the adornment of the palatial residences of our Upper Ten. We doubt if any where in this country, outside of New York city, there can be seen such an extensive and varied assortment of goods in this line. As an example of the magnitude of the business here carried on, we noted one lot of bedsteads numbering 16,000. Other articles seemed to be in like grand proportions.

Every thing about the establishment is very conveniently arranged for the facilitation of business. A Steam Elevator is soon to be put in to aid in the handling of stock, and numerous other improvements, demanded by the growing trade, are in contemplation. We may suggest, by way of inducing persons to visit Hale & Bro's., that their location on the West Side, the domain of comparatively low rents, enables them to give to their customers advantages in the matter of prices that are hardly possible upon this side of the river.

THE WHOLESALE TRADE of Chicago has experienced a truly wonderful growth during the past six years, since the establishment of the national banking system has freed our merchants from the degraded condition of the old Western currency.

THE GROCERY TRADE is of great magnitude. There are over eighty firms engaged exclusively in the wholesale branch of this business, whose sales aggregated last year forty millions of dollars.

THE DRY GOODS TRADE is about equal in amount to the grocery. There are about forty firms engaged in the wholesale branch, whose sales annually foot up between forty and fifty millions; two of whom, last year, exceeded seven million dollars each.

THE WHOLESALE BOOT AND SHOE TRADE.—In the city of Chicago there are engaged in the wholesale manufacture of boots and shoes, some twenty-five houses, whose annual business, as manufacturers alone, amounts to over $2,000,000. This great industry, great not so much for what it now is as for what it promises to be in the future—has been built up within the past twenty years, and in the face of a most vigorous, and at first, apparently ruinous competition with old and well-established Eastern factories, possessed of all the advantages that long experience, abundance of labor-saving machinery and skilled workmen, together with large capital, could give.

Now the wholesale boot and shoe manufacture is one of the fixed facts of Chicago. The business is established upon a sure basis, and is beyond the reach of Eastern competition, for the reason that everywhere in the Western market it is well known that Chicago-made boots and shoes are far superior, both in material and workmanship, to those made elsewhere.

There is no Chicago house deserving of more honor for the achievement of these results, than that of Doggett, Bassett & Hills. The original of the present firm was established in 1846, under the name of Ward & Doggett, and was the first to engage in the wholesale boot and shoe trade in the city. Some four years later, they began to manufacture, and were the pioneers in this also. Messrs. Bassett and Hills having been admitted to the firm, it continued to prosper until 1857, when Mr. Ward died, and the business was continued under the present firm name.

That first year's business, away back in 1846, amounted to about $10,000, and was thought to be a good trade. So it was for the time. That was the "day of small things" with Chicago. Our thoroughfares were then "no thoroughfares," save by the grace of the clerk of the weather, and that despotic character was not gracious for more than one-third of the year. Our entire population at that remote day was only 14,000, and the radius of our trade hardly extended a hundred miles in any direction. The city of LaSalle, now of a population of perhaps 7,000, was then one of our formidable rivals; and there are now in that forlorn looking settlement dozens of owners of lots and blocks, who invested and located there in preference to Chicago, well satisfied that that would be the metropolis, and Chicago probably a thriving town.

Verily, things have changed since then. Chicago has become the home of 300,000 souls, and her wealth, business and influence exhibit a proportionate increase. The men who then staked their fortunes on the future of this city, have grown with its growth, and prospered with its prosperity. Among the more prominent of these, are the gentlemen composing the firm of which we write. They had faith, and, coupled with it, energy, perseverance and integrity. They behold the fruits thereof in a business amounting to some $2,000,000 annually, extending throughout the West and Northwest, requiring, for its conduct, a small army of workmen, clerks, and other employees, and occupying all the floors of the magnificent building located at Nos. 29 and 31 Lake street, and 36 and 38 Wabash avenue.

Mr. Bassett, of the firm, resides at Boston, where, some years ago, an office was opened in connection with the establishment in this city. Mr. B. is therefore personally present in the Eastern market, prepared to take advantage of the fluctuations, and able, with the abundant means at his command, to buy when stock is cheapest. The benefit thus derived to the house is one which it is well disposed to share with its patrons, selling to them at a reasonable advance upon a very moderate cost.

Doggett, Bassett & Hills are not only enterprising and able men in their own proper business, but they are among the leading citizens in Chicago. There are few enterprises of importance which have been set on foot in our city, within the last ten years, in which one or other of the partners, or the house itself, has not invested some capital. And better still, there are fewer of our noble public and private charities which have not been materially assisted by these same gentlemen.

The united sales in this business now exceeds fifteen millions. The number of Eastern shoes sold in this market annually decreasing in the ratio of the capacity of our home manufacture to supply the demand.

The manufactories of Chicago are very considerable, taking into account that it is only within a very few years that the attention of enterprising men of sufficient capital has been directed to building up a manufacturing system commensurate with the requirements of even our present needs. Still, however, a noble beginning has been made, and the returns of last year exhibit over one thousand manufactories of every description, employing a capital of nearly $30,000,000, the estimated value of whose products foot up $70,000,000.

CHICAGO no longer depends upon the New York and Boston Brokers for her supply of teas. The great East India Tea Company, whose elegantly appointed stores are located at No. 116 Clark Street and 83 State Street, through their resident agents in China and Japan, select the very best quality of the new crops for this market, and ship direct to Chicago. The enterprise and spirit of this Company was notably exemplified recently; in their desire to have the honor of being the first direct importers from beyond the Pacific, their first cargo of teas, by the new route across the Continent, was carried, by teams, a distance of twenty miles, to connect by railway, and landed in Chicago several weeks ahead of the final completion of the railroad. They are enabled to sell these choice teas at New York cash prices.

THE FIRST establishment for the manufacture of wall paper was started by Messrs. M. A. Howell, Jr., & Co., whose extensive warerooms are located at Nos. 117 and 119 State street. This firm, whose print works are at Marseilles, in this State, confine themselves exclusively to a wholesale trade, and their productions, on inspection, will be found to embrace the whole range of wall papers and window shades, from the cheapest and plainest to the most costly and elaborate designs and patterns, equal to any imported from England or France.

CALIFORNIA WINES.—The cultivation of the grape on this continent, after many experiments and some discouragements has become a successful and highly profitable business, and now whole sections of the Pacific coast are given up to the culture of the vine. Until very recently the prejudice against native wines was very great, fashion and custom decreeing that none but imported wines were worth drinking. But now the nicest connoiseurs confess, that the California wines, in purity and delicacy of flavor, exceed any of the so-called imported wines in the market. Messrs. Perkins, Stern & Co., the founders of the wine trade in California, and owners of many extensive vineyards, have a branch house in Chicago, at Nos. 34 and 36 La Salle street. They sell nothing but the pure, genuine wines, and from their facilities for securing the choicest products of the State, are enabled to offer superior inducements to parties purchasing at wholesale.

GENT'S FURNISHING HOUSE.—One of the most elegant and complete gents' furnishing establishments in the country is the well known house of J. H. O'Brien, at No. 88 Dearborn street. His stock is always complete in every department in his line of goods. His many years experience in the business and large capital enables him to command the markets of the East, and import his own Irish linens and French lawns. All the materials used are purchased for cash, and manufactured under his own personal supervision, so that any person studying economy may safely rely upon the prices asked being as moderate as any New York house.

In the manufacture of shirts Mr. O'Brien has attained a deserved eminence. Having devoted many years to the study of this, he has reduced it almost to a science, well knowing that no gentleman is really dressed without a well fitting shirt. In under-wear, neck-ties, suspenders, shoulder braces, socks, handkerchiefs, and all the numerous articles which go to make up the necessities of a gentleman's toilet of the day his stock will be found unsurpassed in variety, quality, price, and fashion in Paris, London, or elsewhere. It has been, for years, his ambition to build up an establishment worthy of Chicago; that as she excels in most things, she shall not be distanced by any city in his line of business. That he has succeeded his fellow citizens well know and appreciate, and strangers will have no reason to go elsewhere to be perfectly suited.

SUBURBAN VILLAGES.

THE marvelous advances which our city has made in the extent of dimensions has only been characteristic of its rapidity in the growth of business, and every suburban town established is the living evidence of the city's material prosperity, and the citizen's love of home, comfort, and pleasure. We notice with feelings of pleasure and pride the establishment of towns, villages—nay, almost cities, near this the Metropolis of the West—all the best proof of the prosperity, independence, and comfort of our people. Already Chicago has established on every side—save only where the lake marks her border—homes for her business men.

RAVENSWOOD.

Such is the pretty and attractive name chosen for one of the healthiest and most attractive of the suburban villages. Ravenswood is situated five and one half miles from the Court House, on the line of the Milwaukee division of the Chicago & Northwestern Railroad, twenty minutes ride from the depot, and is supplied with fourteen passenger trains daily. The land is eighteen feet above the level of the North Branch, capable of thorough drainage, and is beautifully diversified with oak groves and evergreens, the latter being plentifully supplied by the company who offer the property for sale.

The tract of ground composing the possessions of the company includes about two hundred and fifty acres of rich, fertile, and easily cultivated soil, formerly well known to the lovers of country attractions as the site of Wood's Nursery. Here, we may note, that although little notice has been publicly made of this most attractive site, the gentlemen owning the land and intended residents are among the most prominent and influential of our citizens, and the assured evidences of its future growth have been so far developed, that already a post office has been established, and the railway has marked Ravenswood among its regular halting places.

We can give no better guarantee of the character and selectness of the enterprise than by mentioning the names of the original projectors. These are Messrs. John M. Wilson, C. T. Bowen, L. A. Willard, C. P. Leland, J. H. Kedzie, L. L. Greenleaf, Merrill Ladd, L. Hodges, and others. These gentlemen, with a view of establishing a worthy suburban home, combining the pleasures and comforts of country life with ready access to city business, became the purchasers of this really beautiful site. Nearly all of them have reserved for themselves elegant lots, as the seats of homes soon to be established. The officers of the company are Daniel A. Jones, President; L. L. Greenleaf, Vice President; J. H. Kedzie and C. T. Bowen, Trustees.

The town is most beautifully laid off, intersected by avenues eighty feet in width, and alleys of twenty feet width. Groves of beautiful foliage adorn the premises, as a natural growth, and cultivation has added most abundantly to the inviting spot. The ready accessibility to Ravenswood constitutes one of its not least inviting features. In addition to the railway communication, the "dummy" on the North Chicago City railroad runs very near the site. On the west of the tract, and very near the same, is Lincoln avenue, a thoroughly well graded road, and very near, on the east, is the Green Bay road. From Lincoln Park to Ravenswood, on the Green Bay road, is an inviting drive.

The village of Ravenswood is already laid off into lots of fifty feet frontage, with a depth of 160 to 170 feet, with, as has been said, streets of eighty feet width and alleys of twenty feet width, intersecting. Each lot is tastefully adorned with trees, evergreens, and shubbery, and no lot will be sold unless the purchaser consents to such adornment and culture. In the center of the tract, and hiding the railway track from obtrusive seeming, is Ravenswood Park, on either side of which are most beautiful and elegant evergreens of gigantic growth. Broad avenues extend in either direction through the village, leading from Lincoln avenue to the Green Bay road, or to the "dummy" on the street railway, each street being lined with trees and evergreens. Every purchaser of a lot is furnished by the company with trees ornamental, and fruit trees and shrubbery, for the adornment of the grounds, and to insure the pleasures of a country home. The company have about fifty thousand evergreen trees in the ground, and are now ready to dispose of the surplus quantity.

Messrs. Hodges and Van Allen, real estate agents, No. 152 Madison street, are the agents for the sale of the property, Mr. Hodges being the actual manager of the company. An inspection of the grounds will amply repay a visit.

WASHINGTON HEIGHTS.

Among the many suburban places around Chicago there is no one more attractive than the new one just laid out on the north end of what is known as Blue Island, a well timbered ridge of the highest elevation of any land within twenty miles of Chicago. This new place is called Washington Heights, and is at the junction (or near it) of the Chicago, Rock Island & Pacific, and the Chicago, Columbus, and Indiana Central railroads. The Rock Island road managers are now grading another road right through the heart of this tract of land, on which they are going to run their dummy train immediately, which will leave the depot of the Rock Island road, on Van Buren, opposite La Salle street, every hour of the day, and will make the fastest time of any accommodation train out of Chicago, making the time from Chicago to Washington Heights in thirty-five minutes. Elegant cars are already made, on purpose to accommodate the rural loving public on this route, and will be placed on the road as soon as the dummy track is ready. The fare will be lower than on any other road running out of the city. The Chicago, Columbus, and Indiana Central road are already running a dummy to and past Washington Heights three times each day, at a fare of seventeen cents for commutation tickets, besides all the regular passenger and freight trains stop at the crossing of the above roads, right in the center of this tract of land, and the fare has recently been reduced to a low figure on all the trains. These facilities for getting in and out of the city at all hours of the day and night, together with the high and beautiful wooded land which commands a fine view of the city and Lake Michigan, will make Washington Heights one of our most attractive suburbs. The facilities for getting there by carriage are also fine, as Halsted street is already graveled within one mile of the place, and will, with the old Vincennes road, in which Halsted street terminates, be graveled to Washington Heights the coming season.

The company owning this new place is called the Blue Island Land and Building company, and received their charter the past winter. The officers are: F. H. Winston, Esq., President, and George D. Walker, Esq., Secretary and Treasurer. Among the principal stockholders are Hon. John F. Tracy, President Rock Island railroad; F. H. Winston, Esq., Attorney for said road; Charles H. Walker, Esq.; John B. Lyon, Esq.; Thos. S. Dobbins, Esq.; L. P. Hilliard, Esq.; Charles W. Weston, Esq.; Charles H. Hopkinson, Esq , and Jas. Millikin, Esq., banker, of Decatur, Ill. Messrs. Clarke, Layton & Co. are the business managers.

Fine grounds are now being fitted up for picnic parties, free of cost to the public, and accommodations by railroad for the same can be had at any time. Beautiful wide avenues are now being constructed by the company, and the tract is being artistically laid off in five and ten acre lots, by Col. J. F. Foster, engineer and landscape surveyor.

ENGLEWOOD.

Englewood continues to attract the attention of real estate dealers and business men in this city generally.

There are three reasons for this, the main one being that Englewood is naturally a delightful residence spot, surrounded by beautiful groves, just the place for the man of business to build his residence, where he may enjoy the pleasures of country surroundings, fresh air, shady groves, green grass for his children, and ground for flowers and gardens — in fact, a place in which to build a perfect *rus in urbe* — at a distance of only six miles from the city. And this last is the second reason for the popularity of Englewood. It is only half an hour from the business centre of the city, by any one of three roads, and its facilities of communication are being increased every day. The third reason is, the inhabitants of the place are enterprising, *live* men, who are determined to do all they can to second nature in making Englewood an agreeable and comfortable residence. They are gathering around them institutions of learning of the very highest class, and otherwise leaving no stone unturned to attract residents to their village.

A very valuable tract of land, situated in this enterprising suburb, has recently been put on the market by Mr. J. P. White, of No. 152 Madison street. This tract consists of thirty-five acres, is known as the Dickey tract, having formerly been the property of Judge Dickey, and is designated as the east thirty-five acres of the north seventy acres of the northwest quarter of section 21, town 39, range 14 east. It is three blocks west of the Rock Island, Michigan Southern, and Fort Wayne railroads, just west of the Female College, and three blocks north of the Normal School tract, comprising the northeast quarter of the tract marked on the map as Linden Grove. The lots are among the finest offered any where in the neighborhood of Chicago. Liberal inducements will be offered to persons desirous of obtaining permanent building sites.

HYDE PARK.

THE village of Hyde Park is the oldest of the suburban villages of Chicago, having been laid out in 1853. It now contains a population of about 2,000 inhabitants. It is about six miles south from the Court House, on the lake shore, and is reached by the Illinois Central Railroad, trains running every hour from the depot, foot of Lake street. Its contiguity to the city, and facility of access, has made Hyde Park the favorite suburb of Chicago. In 1856 Mr. Paul Cornell erected a handsome and spacious hotel, which is conducted in every respect equal to the first hotel in the city. During the summer time this is a favorite resort, and Hyde Park is fast becoming to Chicago what Nahant is to Boston. There are many very elegant residences erected here, and the gardens and grounds exhibit the taste of a refined and cultivated community. There are several churches, and both public and private schools, The South-side Park and Boulevards will add considerably to the attractions of Hyde Park, and very materially advance the value of real estate. W. H. Hoyt & Son, of this city, will furnish every information with regard to real estate in Hyde Park.

THE VILLAGE OF JEFFERSON.

This little town, comparatively unknown as yet, is destined to become one of the finest in the vicinity of Chicago, situated only eight miles from the Court House, and two miles from the city limit, on the Northwestern Railroad. Trains pass this station almost every hour. This point is the terminus of a number of roads, centering here from the surrounding rich and delightful country; one of these running in a due line eastward directly to the Lake, a distance of about three miles. Milwaukee avenue, one of the finest drives leading out of Chicago, also passes through this town. Along the avenue there are many fine country residences, surrounded by beautiful gardens, filled in their season with every kind of fruit, flowers, evergreens, and every thing that the eye delights to feast upon, making this one of the most pleasing drives out of Chicago. The village is located upon ground far above the Lake, thereby rendering it an exception to most of the suburban towns in the vicinity of Chicago.

Of late several gentlemen, having had their attention

called to these superior natural advantages, have made investments here, with the view to greatly improve the the town, and render it one of the choicest and most desirable places for country residence, especially so for the laboring men of Chicago. The number of trains, reduction of the fare, cheapness of rents, and the low price at which lots can be bought, must soon bring the town into general notice. Churches of different denominations are already planted here, schools established, with the necessary hotels and stores, thereby affording every necessary convenience.

There is not a laboring man in Chicago who is not able to secure a home in this most delightful village and pay for it out of his daily wages in a short time. Would it not be wise, then, for all these parties to duly consider this question before the speculative spirit of Chicago has monopolized these now golden opportunities.

Further inquiries will be answered by inquirinfl of Graham, Perry & Co., Room 8 Major Block, corner LaSalle and Madison streets.

EVANSTON

Is a delightful and prosperous town situated on the Milwaukee branch of the Northwestern railroad, twelve miles from the city. It was originally laid out by Dr. Evans, now Governor of Colorado. It is the seat of several eminent institutions of learning, among others the Northwestern Methodist Episcopal University, the Garrett Biblical Institute, and several schools and seminaries of excellent repute. Many of the leading and wealthy citizens of Chicago have built elegant mansions, and here reside with their families. Situated on a high ridge, commanding a magnificent view of the lake and surrounding country, no more desirable place can be selected for a suburban home. The social intercourse is refined and high toned, and the educational advantages unequaled. Some choice lots can still be secured. James M. Kerr & Son, Morrison block, on Clark street, real estate dealers, will furnish every information to parties desiring to locate in this beautiful suburb.

CLASSIFIED LIST

OF

FIRST-CLASS BUSINESS HOUSES IN CHICAGO.

In the following list we present the names of none but first-class houses in their respective lines of business. The stranger visiting the city may rely with implicit confidence upon the representations made to him by any of the houses embraced in the list. The figures in the last column indicate the page upon which the card of the house is printed in this book.

Academy.
Christian Brothers, 99 Van Buren street...................... 74
Adding Machine.
Waite, Charles, Jr., 94 Washington street...................... 8
Architects.
Boyington, W. W., Washington, N. W. cor. Dearborn street 146
Winchell, John K., 129 Dearborn street........................ 206
Art Galleries.
Carbutt, John, 24 Washington street 209
Hovey and Heffron, 53 and 55 State street...................... 145
O'Brien, M., 51 State street................................... 147
McIntyre, Peck & Co., 136 State street.....................8, 151
Opera House, Washington, near State street..................... 203
Attorneys at Law.
Givins & Gilbert, 8 Tribune Building.......................... 206
Awnings, Tents, Tarpaulins, Etc.
Gilbert Hubbard & Co., 205 and 207 S. Water street 181
Baking Powders.
Royal Baking Powder Co., Agency 185 S. Water street........... 193
Banks and Bankers.
First National Bank, State, S. W. cor. Washington street......... 108
Greenebaum, Henry & Co., Lake, S. W. cor. La Salle street..... 184
Hibernian Banking Association, Lake, S. W. cor. Clark.......... 183
National Loan and Trust Co., La Salle, cor. Washington street.. 184
Smith, George C. & Bro., La Salle, cor. Washington street....... 184
The Marine Company of Chicago, Lake, cor. La Salle street...... 185

Van Deursen, W. P. & Co,. 106 La Salle street..................... 192
Winslow, Ferd. S., 2 S. Clark street 186

Boot and Shoe Manufacturers.

Doggett, Bassett & Hills, 29 and 81 Lake st. and 86 and 88
    Wabash av...161, 180

Breweries.

Sands' Ale Brewing Co., Pearson, cor. Pine St.................... 194

California Wines.

Perkins, Stern & Co, 84 and 86 La Salle street 190

Clothing.

Belding, G. T., 96 and 98 Randolph............................... 200

Commission Merchants.

Scanlan & Fitzgibbon, (General) 191 S. Water street............. 204
Sturges, McAllister & Co., (Woolen and Cotton Goods) 80 and 82
    Wabash av.. 216

Confectionery Manufacturers.

Page, M. E. & Co., 24 Michigan av................................ 202
Scanlan Bros. & Colburn, 78 State street......................... 204

Dry Goods, Wholesale.

Farwell, John V. & Co., 42, 44 and 46 Wabash avenue............. 221
Field, Palmer & Leiter, State, N. E. cor. Washington street...... 159
Bowen, Whitman & Winslow... 219

Druggists, Wholesale.

Dwyer, E. P. & Co., 92 and 94 Lake street........................ 18
Lord & Smith.. 217

Engravers on Wood.

Maas & Mantz, Reynolds' Block 206

European Freight Express.

Webster's Express, Chamber of Commerce........................... 187

European Passage Offices.

Greenebaum, H. & Co., La Salle, cor. Lake street................. 184
Hibernian Banking Association, Lake, S. W. cor. Clark street.... 183
Rowe, S., Adams House, Lake, N. W. cor. Michigan avenue......... 190
Winslow, Ferd. S., 2 S. Clark street............................. 186

Fancy Groceries.

Scanlan Bros. & Colburn, 78 State street 204

Fine Art Goods.

McIntyre, Peck & Co., 186 State street........................... 8
O'Brien, M., 51 State street..................................... 147

Fire Extinguisher.

Northwestern Fire Extinguisher Co., 122 Washington street 207

Foreign Exchange Dealers.

Greenebaum, Henry & Co., Lake, cor. Lasalle street.............. 184
National Loan & Trust Co., La Salle, cor. Washington street..... 184
The Marine Company of Chicago, Lake, cor. La Salle street....... 185
Winslow, Ferd. S., 2 S. Clark street............................. 186

Business Houses.

Freight Agents.
Walsh, J. & Co., Chamber of Commerce........................ 187

Gents' Furnishing Goods.
Witkowsky, D. Sr., 64 and 66 Randolph and 66, 68 and 70 State st. 181

Grocers, Wholesale.
Doane, J. W. & Co., 49 and 51 Michigan avenue 193

Hardware, General and Building.
Wayne, J. L. & Son, 190 Lake street 208

Hats, Caps and Furs.
Keith Brothers... 218

Hotels.
Briggs House, Randolph, cor. Wells street..................... 188
Laclede Hotel, W. Madison, cor. Canal street.................. 198
Tremont House, Dearborn and Lake streets 187

India Pale Ale and Lager-Beer Brewers.
Sands' Ale Brewing Co., Pearson, cor. Pine street 196

Insurance Companies.
Commercial Insurance Company, 162 Washington street......... 111
Home Insurance Company, Pope's Block......................... 119
Merchants Insurance Company, La Salle, cor. Washington st.105, 110
Putnam Life Insurance Company................................ 115
Republic Insurance Company.................................... 117
Phœnix Insurance Company..................................... 118
Firemens Insurance Company, La Salle, cor. Washington street.. 114
Washington Life, La Salle, cor. Washington street............. 117

Labor Exchange.
Hunter & Wood, 92 Randolph street............................ 197

Medical Institutes.
Chicago Hotel for Invalids, S. Clark, cor. Jackson street 99
Chicago Eye and Ear Infirmary, Reynolds Block 100
Dr. Justin Hayes.. 98
Dr. Trine's Movement Cure, 186 State street 195

Merchant Tailors
Belding, G. T. & Co., 96 and 98 Randolph street................ 200
Brown & Matthews, 93 Wabash avenue......................... 180
Witkowsky, D., Sr., 64 and 66 Randolph, and 66, 68 and 70 State streets.. 214

Ocean Steamship Lines.
Allan Line, (Ferd. S. Winslow, Agent) 2 S. Clark street.......... 186
Cunard Line, office Adams House, Lake st. cor. Michigan avenue. 190
National Steamship Line, 16 Chamber of Commerce............ 187

Paints, Oils and Glass.
Dwyer, E. P. & Co., 92 and 94 Lake street...................... 18

Parlor Billiard Tables.
McIntyre, Peck & Co., 186 State street......................... 8

Pawnbrokers.
Goldsmid, A. & Co., 281 Clark street........................... 216

Business Houses.

Photograph Galleries.
Carbutt's, 24 Washington street................................. 209
Hall's, 122 Lake street.... 210

Piano Forte Dealers.
Sea, S. W. & Co., Portland Block................................. 211

Planing Mill.
Russell, S. I., Fulton, near Jefferson street................... 155

Produce and Commission Merchants.
Scanlan & Fitzgibbon, 191 S. Water street.................... 204

Railway and Transportation Lines.
Michigan Southern R. R., Ticket office under Sherman House; Depot, Van Buren, opposite La Salle street................ 188
Goodrich Line, Office, dock below Rush street bridge......... 195, 191
Union Pacific Railroad, 72 La Salle street......................... 189

Real Estate Dealers.
Averill, J. A., 7 Metropolitan Block. 215
Baird & Bradley, 90 La Salle street................................ 6
Banker, Bros. & Greene, 131 La Salle street.................... 6
Boyden, N. B., 106 Madison street................................ 206
Boyden & Grierson, 94 La Salle street........................... 4
Bragg, F. A. & Co., 120 Dearborn street......................... 208
Burchell, J. E. & Co., 122 Washington street................... 207
Chandler, J. B., 125 Dearborn street.............................. 208
Clark, Streeter & Co., 122 Washington street 7
Clarke, Layton & Co., 128 Washington street................. 2
De Loynes & Parent, 2 Major Block...............................
Gaubert, C. H. & Co., 144 Madison street......................
Givins & Gilbert, 8 Tribune Building.............................. 206
Graham, Perry & Co., Major Block................................ 218
Higginson, G. M., 7 Metropolitan Block 215
Hitt, Hardin & Hitt, 10 Tribune Building......................... 206
Hodges & Van Allen, Major Block..... 167
Hubbard & Jackson, 121 Dearborn street.. 215
Illinois Central R. R. Land Department, 53 Michigan avenue..... 223
Kerfoot, S. H. & Co., 71 Dearborn street 219
Kerfoot, W. D., 87 Washington street..........................Back cover
Kerr, J. M. & Son, Morrison Block 169
Kinzie Bros., 104 Madison street 3
Mann & Day, 17 Tribune Building................................. 195
Norris, G. H. & Co., 128 Lake street. 211
Olinger, Waller & Co., 7 Union Building 8
Phare, W. H. & Co., 115 Dearborn street....................... 12
Rice & Wadsworth, 87 Washington street 208
Scoville & Harvey, 1 Metropolitan Block 220
Snyder & Lee, 4 Metropolitan Block............................... 5
White, J. P., 152 Madison street................................... 168
Waite, Geo. W. & Son, 9 Tribune Building..................... 215
Warren & Goodrich, 125 Dearborn street 6

Restaurants.
Collins & McGuire, 119 Dearborn street......................... 139
Smith and Odlin, 81 Clark street... 141

Business Houses.

Savings' Banks.
Hibernian Banking Association, Lake, S. W. cor. Clark street.... 183
Merchant's, Farmer's and Mechanic's Bank, 13 Clark street 105

Scales and Balances.
Fairbanks', 226 and 228 Lake street............................ 211
Sampson Scale Co., Lake, N. W. cor. La Salle street............ 212

School Furniture.
Andrews, A. H. & Co , 111 State street......................... 16

Ship Chandlers.
Gilbert Hubbard & Co., 205 and 207 S. Water street 181

Tea and Coffee Importers.
East India Tea Company, 83 State and 116 Clark streets..... 163, 216

Theatre.
Aiken's Dearborn Theatre 105

Ticket Offices.
Rowe, S., Adams House, Lake, cor. Michigan avenue 190

Tintypes and Ferrotypes.
Hall's Gallery, 122 Lake street................................ 210

Transfer and Shipping Agent.
Walsh, J. & Co., 16 Chamber of Commerce 198

Transportation Company.
Goodrich Transportation Co., Office on Docks, below Rush street
  bridge..191, 193
Webster's European Freight Line, 16 Chamber of Commerce....... 187

Twines and Cordage.
Gilbert Hubbard & Co., 205 and 207 S. Water street 181

Vinegar Manufacturers.
Prussing, C. G. E., 339 and 341 State street................... 193
Weigle, Fred., 189 and 191 S. Canal street 204

Wall Paper Manufacturers.
Howell, M. A. Jr., & Co., 117 and 119 Wabash avenue............ 179

Watches and Jewelry.
Tobin, B. F., 135 Clark street................................. 169

Water and Gas Pipe Manufactories.
Walworth, Twohig & Furse, 225 Lake street...................... 195

Wines and Liquors.
Mann, Shears & Co., 53 S. Water street......................... 196
Myers, Sam'l & Co., 268 and 270 Madison street 204

Woolen and Cotton Goods, Commission.
Sturgis, McAllister & Co., 80 and 82 Wabash avenue............. 216

Wool Dealers, Commission.
Sturgis, McAllister & Co., 80 and 82 Wabash avenue............. 216

Wrought Iron and Brass Tubing, etc.
Walworth, Twohig & Furse, 225 Lake street...................... 159

C. H. Gaubert & Co.,

REAL ESTATE

AND

LOAN AGENTS,

Room 1, Stone's Building, 144 Madison Street,

CHICAGO, ILLS.

HOUSES AND LOTS BOUGHT AND SOLD ON COMMISSION.

LOANS NEGOTIATED.   HOUSES RENTED.

RENTS COLLECTED.

TAXES PAID FOR NON-RESIDENTS.

Prompt and reliable information given.

We invite Correspondence and Inquiry Personally or by Letter.

We have a large list of VALUABLE PROPERTY FOR SALE, to which the attention of the public is respectfully directed.

C. H. GAUBERT & CO.

ESTABLISHED IN NEW YORK, 1838.

M. A. HOWELL, Jr., & CO.,

MANUFACTURERS OF

WALL PAPER

The only Print Works in the West.

WAREHOUSE:

117 and 119 State Street,   CHICAGO.

PRINT WORKS AT MARSEILLES, ILL.

Doggett, Bassett & Hills,

MANUFACTURERS AND JOBBERS OF

BOOTS & SHOES,

Have now received their NEW SPRING STOCK, which they offer to the Trade at the LOWEST MARKET PRICES.

MANUFACTURE IN CHICAGO

Custom-Made Boots and Shoes of Superior Quality,

And keep on hand the LARGEST STOCK of Goods in their line to be found in the West.

FACTORY AND SALESROOMS:

29 & 31 Lake St., and 36 & 38 Wabash Av., CHICAGO.

ORDERS CAREFULLY ATTENDED TO.

Brown & Mathews,

MERCHANT TAILORS,

IMPORTERS OF

FINE WOOLENS FOR MEN'S WEAR,

No. 93 Wabash Ave.,

CHICAGO, ILL.

G. HUBBARD.   GEO. B. CARPENTER.

GILBERT HUBBARD & CO.,

SHIP CHANDLERS
AND DEALERS IN
TWINES AND CORDAGE,

205 & 207 South Water St., - - CHICAGO.

We would call particular attention of the Trade to our Stock, as we at all times have the largest and best assortment in the West of

Cotton and Flax Duck, all Widths,
DITCHING ROPES, MANILLA AND TARRED ROPE,
Bags, Bagging, Burlaps, Canvas, Oakum, Tar, Pitch, Tackle Blocks, Chains, Coal Tar, Roofing Pitch and Felting.

WIRE ROPE, EITHER IRON OR STEEL,
FOR MINING, HOISTING, OR FERRY PURPOSES.

Tents of every kind, Tarpaulins, Awnings, Wagon Covers of Plain or Rubber-Coated Duck.

FLAGS!

Of Silk or Bunting, as per Army Regulations, constantly on hand or made to order.

W. P. Van Deursen & Co.,　　　　Swan & Payson,
　　Chicago, Ill.　　　　　　　50 Wall St., N.Y.

W. P. VAN DEURSEN & CO.,
BANKERS AND BROKERS

106 LaSalle St., **CHICAGO.**

SWAN & PAYSON,

50 Wall Street, New York,

BUY AND SELL, ON COMMISSION,

Railroad Stocks, Bonds, Government Securities, Gold, Express, Telegraph and Miscellaneous Stocks, at the

STOCK EXCHANGE IN NEW YORK,

ON MARGINS,

AT NEW YORK RATES OF COMMISSION AND INTEREST.

NOTES.

Acceptances or other obligations paid by telegraph the same day in New York that Deposit is made with them in Chicago.

LOANS NEGOTIATED.

HIBERNIAN
BANKING ASSOCIATION
SAVINGS BANK,

Southwest Corner Lake and Clark Sts., - CHICAGO.

Receive Money on Deposit and allow Interest thereon.

FOREIGN EXCHANGE.

Drafts on the HIBERNIA BANK of Ireland, and its Branches, in sums to suit, of £1 Sterling and upwards.

PASSAGE TICKETS issued to and from all points in Europe.

OFFICE HOURS:—10 a.m. to 8 p.m.; also, Saturdays, 6 to 8 p.m.

NATIONAL LOAN & TRUST COMPANY,

BANKERS,

Court House Square, cor. LaSalle and Washington Sts.,
CHICAGO.

GEO. C. SMITH & BRO.,
SAME OFFICE.

SPECIALTY OF COLLECTING.

BANK OF DEPOSIT & DISCOUNT.

FOREIGN EXCHANGE.

WE DRAW ON

England, France, Sweden, Norway, Denmark; In Germany, on Frankfort, Stuttgart, Leipzig, Berlin, Bremen, Cologne.

Letters of Credit for Travelers on the American House of DREXEL, HARJES & CO., Paris.

GOLD DRAFTS ON NEW YORK AND CANADA.

HENRY GREENEBAUM & CO.

BANKERS.

THE OLDEST ESTABLISHED BANKING HOUSE IN CHICAGO.

We transact a legitimate Banking Business, Receive Deposits on Current Accounts, Discount to Depositors at bank rates, and Issue

DRAFTS AND LETTERS OF CREDIT

On New York, Boston, Philadelphia, Pittsburg, Cincinnati, St. Louis and Milwaukee; also on San Francisco, Cal., and the principal cities in Great Britain and Ireland, Norway and Sweden, Holland, France, Italy, Switzerland and Germany. Issue Passage Orders from and to all European Ports, by Steam and Sailing Vessels.

We shall be happy to receive applications from responsible parties at all desirable points to enter into arrangements with us for the sale of our Exchange on our correspondents abroad.

Travelers to Europe can procure of the undersigned LETTERS OF CREDIT available throughout England, France, Germany, Switzerland, Italy, etc., thus incurring the expense of premium on gold only on the amount actually used while abroad.

THE MARINE COMPANY.

OF CHICAGO.

Office, Cor. Lake and La Salle Sts.

CAPITAL, - - - $500,000.
ASSETS, - - - $507,434.27.

J. YOUNG SCAMMON, President.
JOHN M. UNDERWOOD, Vice-Pres.
SAMUEL S. ROGERS, Secretary.
EUGENE C. LONG, Treasurer.

GENERAL BANKING AND EXCHANGE.

Allow Interest on Savings and Trust Deposits.

Sell Drafts for £1 and over on LONDON; also on the following Cities and Towns in Ireland, viz:
DUBLIN, CORK, LIMERICK, LONDONDERRY, BELFAST, WATERFORD, GALWAY, ATHLONE, KILKENNY, BALLINA AND ENNISKILLEN.

DRAW ALSO ON

PARIS, BERLIN, FRANKFORT, HAMBURG, BREMEN, GENEVA, BASLE, ZURICH, COLOGNE, AND KŒNIGSBERG.

Persons proposing to visit Europe, Egypt, or the Holy Land, can make as satisfactory arrangements for Letters of Credit with this institution as at the East.

ROBERT REID, Manager.

OCEAN STEAMSHIPS.

ALLAN LINE

OF OCEAN STEAMERS.

The Montreal Ocean Steamship Company's

POWERFUL MAIL STEAMERS,

Sailing Every Saturday

FROM QUEBEC FOR LIVERPOOL,

Calling at Londonderry to land passengers and mails. Eighteen first-class Steamers. Most direct and convenient route for travelers to Europe.

Railway fare to Quebec same as to New York. Fare from Quebec to Liverpool, first-class, $80 and $70 gold, according to position of sleeping cabins, all having the same privilege in the saloons.

Tourists' tickets at reduced prices.

Steerage passage, $30 currency. Passage certificates from Europe to all points in the Northwest at cheapest rates. Regular physicians employed on all steamers.

Apply to H. & A. ALLAN, in Montreal, or at the

GENERAL WESTERN AGENCY,

No. 2 South Clark St., Chicago,

Where cabin plans may be seen and berths secured for any steamer.

FERD. S. WINSLOW.

FINANCIAL.

FERD. S. WINSLOW,

FOREIGN BANKING OFFICE

No. 2 South Clark Street, Loomis Building,

SELLS GOLD AND GOLD CHECKS ON NEW YORK AT NEW YORK RATES,

Drafts for sale, in sums to suit, on England, France, Germany, Scandinavia, &c.

NATIONAL STEAM SHIP COMPANY.
(LIMITED.)

BRITISH STEAM SHIPS.

LOUISIANA	2,166 Tons,	ENGLAND	3,450 Tons,
VIRGINIA	2,875 "	ERIN	3,310 "
QUEEN	3,517 "	HELVETIA	3,315 "
DENMARK	3,117 "	PENNSYLVANIA	2,872 "
	FRANCE	3,880 Tons,	

Sail from NEW YORK every SATURDAY, from Pier 47, North River.

Accommodations for Passengers good as—if not superior—to any other Line.

FARES:

Cabin—New York to Liverpool	$100
" " " and Return	180
Steerage	30

Through Bills of Lading given from all parts in the Northwest to Liverpool, London, Glasgow, Dublin, Belfast and Londonderry; and Time guaranteed through to Liverpool in THIRTY days, *via*

"WEBSTER'S EUROPEAN FREIGHT LINE."

S. T. WEBSTER, General Western Agent,
16 Chamber of Commerce, Chicago, Ill.

F. W. J. HURST, Manager,
69 Broadway, New York.

W. B. MACALISTER, General Manager,
LIVERPOOL.

CHANGE OF TIME.

FROM and AFTER

APRIL 26,

EXPRESS TRAINS,

WILL LEAVE

Chicago for Buffalo,

VIA

MICHIGAN SOUTHERN

AND

LAKE SHORE RAILWAY,

AS FOLLOWS:

8:00 a.m., 5:15 and 9:00 p.m.

The only line running through trains between Chicago and Buffalo in direct connection with New York Central and Erie Railway.

The 5:15 P.M. train leaves Chicago daily. All trains stop at Twenty-Second St. to take and leave passengers.

F. E. MORSE,
Gen. Passenger Agent.

RAILROAD FROM THE ATLANTIC to the PACIFIC.

GRAND OPENING
OF THE
UNION PACIFIC RAILROAD.

PASSENGER TRAINS LEAVE

On the Arrival of Trains from the East.

THROUGH to SAN FRANCISCO
In less than Four days, avoiding the Dangers of the Sea!

Travelers for Pleasure, Health or Business,
Will find a trip over the Rocky Mountains Healthy and Pleasant.

LUXURIOUS CARS AND EATING HOUSES
ON THE UNION PACIFIC RAILROAD.

PULLMAN'S PALACE SLEEPING CARS
RUN WITH ALL THROUGH PASSENGER TRAINS.

GOLD, SILVER AND OTHER MINERS!
Now is the time to seek your Fortunes in Nebraska, Wyoming, Arizona, Washington, Dakotah, Colorado, Utah, Oregon, Montana, New Mexico, Idaho, Nevada or California.

CONNECTIONS MADE AT
Cheyenne for Denver, Central City and Santa Fe,
AT OGDEN AND CORINNE FOR HELENA,
BOISE CITY, VIRGINIA CITY, SALT LAKE CITY & ARIZONA.

Through Tickets for sale at all principal Railroad Offices.
Be Sure they Read via Platte Valley or Omaha.

Company's Office 72 La Salle St., opposite City Hall and Court House Square, CHICAGO. **CHAS. E. NICHOLS, Ticket Agent.**
JOHN P. HART, Gen'l Trav. Agent, 72 La Salle St., Chicago; H. BROWNSON, Gen'l Freight Agent, Omaha, Neb.; J. BUDD, Gen'l Ticket Agent, Omaha, Neb.; W. SNYDER, Gen'l Supt., Omaha, Neb.

Cunard Line of Mail Steamers,
BETWEEN NEW YORK AND LIVERPOOL,
CALLING AT QUEENSTOWN.

AUSTRALASIAN,	MALTA,
ALEPPO,	PALMYRA,
CHINA,	SAMARIA,
CUBA,	SIBERIA,
HECLA,	TARIFA,
JAVA,	TRIPOLI.

One of the above First-Class Iron Mail Steamers are intended to sail as follows:

From LIVERPOOL, (calling at Cork Harbor) for NEW YORK DIRECT every SATURDAY.

From LIVERPOOL, (calling at Cork Harbor) for NEW YORK via. BOSTON every TUESDAY.

From NEW YORK for LIVERPOOL, (calling at Cork Harbor) every THURSDAY.

Certificates issued to bring out Passengers from any part of Europe at Lowest Rates.

For Passage apply to E. CUNARD, Trinity Building, 111 Broadway, New York, or to

S. ROWE,
Adams House, Corner Michigan Ave. and Lake Street, CHICAGO.

PERKINS, STERN & CO.'S
CALIFORNIA WINES.

We guarantee the absolute purity of all our Wines.

Being the PIONEER HOUSE, and owning the vineyards from which nearly all our Wines come, we are able to offer them at LOWER PRICES than good genuine Wines can be sold for by any other House.

As founders of the Wine trade in California, we have, in addition to our own extensive vineyards, superior facilities for securing the choicest products of the State.

We would ask especial attention to the fact that *our House is the only one officially endorsed by the California Wine Growers' Association.* Also, to the following, from the *United States Senators from California*:

"We are satisfied that the firm of PERKINS, STERN & Co. sell only genuine California Wines."
C. COLE,
JOHN CONNESS.

☞ We would particularly caution the public against inferior and fictitious articles sold under the name of California Wines, and ask that we be judged by no Wines but our own.

Be sure and ask for PERKINS, STERN & Co.'s California Wines.

34 & 36 La Salle Street.
Represented by **BENJAMIN BRUCE, Jr.**

1869. **1869.**

Goodrich Transportation Company.

SIDE-WHEEL
STEAM BOAT LINES.

NEW PASSENGER STEAMERS
MANITOWOC AND SHEBOYGAN,
Leave Alternately,

FOR MILWAUKEE,

RACINE, SHEBOYGAN,

Port Washington, Manitowoc and Two Rivers.

Every Morning, Sundays excepted, at 9 o'clock.

The same Steamers leave MILWAUKEE for CHICAGO, alternately, at 7 P. M., DAILY.

Saturday's Boat leaves for MILWAUKEE at 8 P. M.

TUESDAY EVENINGS and FRIDAY MORNINGS, Boats go through to KEWAUNEE and AHNEPEE, stopping at all other Points named above.

FARE, Meals and Berths Included :

TO RACINE,	$1 50	TO MANITOWOC	4 00
" MILWAUKEE	2 00	" TWO RIVERS	4 00
" PT. WASHINGTON	3 00	" KEWAUNEE	5 00
" SHEBOYGAN	3 50	" AHNEPEE	5 00

TRAVELING BY THE BOATS, (Board included,) CHEAPER THAN STAYING AT HOME.

Fare (Meals and Berths included) $1.00 less than by Rail.

ALL RAILROAD TICKETS GOOD ON THE BOATS.

Fare to Milwaukee, (Meals included,) only $2.00.

Shippers can rely on prompt dispatch of all goods delivered up to 8 o'clock A. M.

STEAMERS ORION AND ALPENA
WILL LEAVE CHICAGO
FOR GRAND HAVEN & MUSKEGON,

Alternately, every Evening, at 7 o'clock, Sundays excepted.
(Arriving at Grand Haven in time for Morning Trains,)

For Grand Rapids and Saginaw,
And all Stations on D. & M. R. R.; also Connecting with

ENGELMANN'S DAILY LINE STEAMERS,
For White Hall, Stoney Creek, Pent Water, Ludington and Manistee.

Returning, will leave MUSKEGON every Afternoon, and GRAND HAVEN every Evening, on arrival of Trains from Detroit.

FARE LESS THAN BY ANY OTHER ROUTES.

FOR ST. JOSEPH,

The Speedy Side-Wheel Steamer, COMET,

Will leave for ST. JOSEPH every day, (Sundays excepted,) at 10 o'clock. SATURDAY'S Boat will not leave until 11 o'clock at night.

Returning, will leave ST. JOSEPH every Evening, (Saturdays excepted,) at 10 o'clock.

FOR GREEN BAY AND MENOMONEE,
And all Intermediate Points,
STEAMERS TRUESDELL AND ST. JOSEPH—Semi-Weekly.

Truesdell Leaves Every Tuesday Evening, at 7 o'clock.

Fare,---Meals and Berths Included :
To Washington Harbor, Bailey's Harbor, Fish Creek, Green Bay and Menomonee......... $6 00

GOODRICH'S OMNIBUS LINE

Will convey Passengers and their Baggage to all Hotels and Depots for 50 cents. Baggage checked from Boats to all Hotels and Depots, and also to any part of the City at Lowest Rates.

☞ *All Goods for above named Ports, should be delivered at* GOODRICH'S STEAMBOAT LANDING. For further Information, Freight or Passage, apply to

A. E. GOODRICH, President.

Docks below Rush Street Bridge.

J. W. DOANE &
WHOLESALE GROCERS,

49 & 51 Michigan Avenue,

CHICAGO.

PRUSSING'S
CELEBRATED
Cider Vinegar.

A SPLENDID ARTICLE.

Warranted Pure, and to Preserve Pickles.

First Premium awarded at the U. S. Fair, the Illinois State Fair, and Chicago City Fair.

Largest Works of the kind in the United States.

CHARLES G. E. PRUSSING,

339 & 341 State Street, Chicago.

Ask your Grocer for Prussing's Vinegar.

Royal Baking Powder
COMPANY.

Capital - - - - **$100,000**

60 VESEY STREET, NEW YORK.

C. A. HOAGLAND, President.   J. C. HOAGLAND, Secretary.
F. H. HALL, Vice-President.   WM. M. CLARKE, Gen'l Agent.

Western Office: 135 South Water Street,

CHICAGO, ILLS.

SANDS'
ALE BREWING COMPANY

Fred. A. Wheeler, Secretary.

Corner of Pearson and Pine Streets,

CHICAGO, ILLS.

BREWERS OF

INDIA PALE ALES, STOCK ALES,

PORTERS AND LAGER BEER.

WALWORTH, TWOHIG & FURSE,

Wrought Iron, Brass and Galvanized
TUBING,

BRASS AND IRON FITTINGS,

Locomotive, Marine and Stationary
BOILERS AND ENGINES,

STEAM WARMING AND VENTILATING APPARATUS.

OFFICE and WAREHOUSE, 225 Lake St., } **CHICAGO.**
FACTORY, Franklin, Cor. Michigan,

S. H. MANN.   S. D. DAY.

LOAN and REAL ESTATE OFFICE.
MANN & DAY,
17 TRIBUNE BUILDING, CHICAGO, ILL.

Buy, Sell, or Exchange, all kinds of Real Estate, in City or Country; Pay Taxes; also Negotiate Loans on Real Estate Securities, and buy short Business Paper.

REFERENCES:—Hon. J. Y. Scammon, Chicago; M. D. Ogden, Esq., Chicago; Hon. B. W. Raymond, Chicago; Messrs. Root & Cady, Chicago.

DRS. J. G. & T. H. TRINE'S
MOVEMENT CURE,
136 STATE STREET.

Dyspeptics, Consumptives, Paralytics, those suffering from Neuralgia, Rheumatism, Constipation, and all cases of Spinal Curvature and Female Weakness, will find the Movement Cure the most appropriate, safe, certain, and agreeable means of restoration.

☞ Call or send for Illustrated Circular.

MANN, SHEARS & CO.,

Importers and Jobbers in

WINES, BRANDIES,

GINS, RUMS,

And Dealers in

FINE KENTUCKY WHISKEYS,

53 South Water Street,

CHICAGO.

We make a specialty of

OLD COPPER DISTILLED WHISKEYS,

From Bourbon, Nelson, Woodford and Anderson Counties, Kentucky.

NORTH WESTERN
LABOR EXCHANGE AGENCY

AND

Chicago Information and Garden City Guide.

OFFICE:

92 EAST RANDOLPH STREET.

Established in 1868.

BEST MALE OR FEMALE HELP FURNISHED,

ON SHORT NOTICE,

To Farmers, Merchants, Manufacturers,

CONTRACTORS AND HOUSEKEEPERS.

SITUATIONS FOUND

For all parties desiring employment.

INFORMATION GIVEN UPON ALL SUBJECTS.

BRANCH OFFICES

In New York, Boston, Detroit and Cincinnati.

HUNTER & WOOD,

92 East Randolph Street, CHICAGO.

J. WALSH & CO.,
General Transfer and Shipping Agents,
16 CHAMBER OF COMMERCE.

Property consigned to our care will be promptly delivered in any part of the city, or transferred to any Railway Depot or Steamboat Dock, and the lowest rates of freight and insurance secured for shippers. Bills of Lading made to shippers and consignees.

JAMES WALSH!,
AGENT
North-Western Union and Northern Packet Line,
16 Chamber of Commerce, - CHICAGO.

LACLEDE HOTEL,
J. A. SAMPLE, PROP'R,
Corner Madison and Canal Sts., CHICAGO, ILL.

This new and commodious House is now open to the public. It is one of the best and most conveniently located Hotels in the city, being directly opposite the

PITTSBURG & FORT WAYNE AND CHICAGO & ST. LOUIS DEPOTS.

The building is a new brick, constructed on the most approved plans, and finished up with all modern improvements. It is complete and handsomely furnished with all New Furniture, Carpets and Spring Beds, and has all the conveniences of a

FIRST CLASS HOTEL.

Persons stopping at this House are assured that every attention will be shown them that may add to their pleasure and comfort.

B. F. TOBIN,
Dealer in

FINE WATCHES, JEWELRY,

Diamonds, Silver Goods, Gold Pens, Spectacles, &c.

AGENT FOR AMERICAN WATCHES.

Sign of the Golden Eagle,

135 CLARK ST., - COR. OF MADISON,
CHICAGO.

REPAIRING ACCURATELY DONE.

G. T. BELDING & CO.,

Manufacturers of and Dealers in

Men's, Boy's and Youth's Ready-Made

CLOTHING!

96 & 98 RANDOLPH ST.,

COR. DEARBORN.

Clothing Made to Order

ON SHORT NOTICE.

(*See next page.*)

M. E. PAGE.   R. P. PATTISON.

M. E. PAGE & CO.

WHOLESALE

CONFECTIONERS!

24 MICHIGAN AVENUE,

Manufacturers of

Rock Candy,

GUM,

CREAM AND CORDIAL WORK.

The Confectionery House of this firm, a cut of which appears on the opposite page, is the largest and most complete concern of the kind in the United States. They occupy the whole of the immense building for the different departments of their business, and have spared no expense in arranging it for turning out the different descriptions of Confectionery manufactured by them, in the most complete and expeditious manner. The firm employ from 70 to 80 hands constantly, their daily consumption of sugar being from 30 to 40 barrels, and their annual sales will exceed a half million of dollars. The firm pride themselves on using nothing but the choicest brands of Loaf and A sugars, and their goods have an extensive and well known reputation for their purity and delicious flavors.

A visit to their establishment, where you will be kindly received by one of the gentlemanly proprietors of the concern, will repay the time and trouble taken. (*See page* 201.)

Opera House Art Gallery,

CHICAGO, ILLINOIS,

AITKEN & FULLER, - - PROPRIETORS.

"The Art Journal,"

An American Review of the Fine Arts.

CHICAGO:

PUBLISHED BY J. F. AITKEN & CO.

OPERA HOUSE ART GALLERY.

CABINET MAKERS' HARDWARE.

UPHOLSTERERS' GOODS — MECHANICS' TOOLS.

J. L. WAYNE,
J. L. WAYNE, Jr.

J. L. WAYNE & SON,
BUILDING & GENERAL HARDWARE,
190 LAKE ST., COR. WELLS,
CHICAGO.

Represented by CARLETON WHITE.

COFFIN GOODS, TRIMMINGS, ETC.

AGENTS FOR THE SALE OF
AMERICAN BURIAL CASES.

EXCELSIOR VINEGAR WORKS.
FREDERICK WEIGLE, PROP'R,

Manufacturer of Cider, Pickle and Double

VINEGAR,

Nos. 189 & 191 S. CANAL ST. Cor. Jackson, CHICAGO.

All Vinegar guaranteed Pure, and to keep Pickles in all instances, and of such strength as desired and agreed upon. First Premiums have been awarded for my brands of Vinegar wherever exhibited.

SCANLAN BRO. & COLBURN,
STEAM
MANUFACTURING CONFECTIONERS!

AND WHOLESALE DEALERS IN
FANCY GROCERIES, CIGARS, &C.

78 STATE STREET,   -   -   CHICAGO.

MORTIMER SCANLAN.   J. J. FITZGIBBON.

SCANLAN & FITZGIBBON,
Produce and General
Commission Merchants,

191 SOUTH WATER ST., CHICAGO.

Particular attention given to the sale of Provisions, Flour, Grain, Dried and Green Fruits, &c.

SAM'L MYERS & CO.,
DISTILLERS OF
RYE MALT WHISKY,
ALCOHOL AND PURE SPIRITS,

Also, Manufacturers of WHITE WINE AND CIDER VINEGAR, and Dealers in Imported Liquors,

268 and 270 East Madison St., (P.O. Box 188) *CHICAGO.*
Rye Whisky of our own distillation, three and four years old.

AIKEN'S
DEARBORN THEATRE,
111 & 113 DEARBORN STREET,
Bet. Madison & Washington.

FRANK E. AIKEN, SOLE LESEE & MANAGER.

This new and beautiful Temple of the Drama, opened on the 18th of January last, by FRANK E. AIKEN, and his Comedy Company, acknowledged by the Press and Public to be

THE THEATRE OF THE WEST!

Is now in the full tide of success, and nightly presenting

NEW AND ELEGANT PLAYS

To Crowded and Delighted Audiences.

THE COMPANY

Is the same that, for the past five years, was at the Museum in this city, when that establishment was open and under the management of FRANK E. AIKEN, and are all recognized

FAVORITES.

ADMISSION ....*50 Cents*
Reserved Seat in Dress Circle ....*75 Cents*
Stalls, Orchestra Circle and Balcony *$1.00*
Family Circle ....*30 Cents*
Private Boxes ....*$5.00 and $6.00*

Admission to Matinee ....*30 Cents*
Reserved Seats ....*50 Cents*
Private Boxes ....*$2.00 and $3.00*

Evening Performance commences at quarter before Eight—Afternoon Performance commences at half-past Two.

RESERVED SEATS can be procured at the principal Hotels, and at the Box Office, from 9 A. M. to 10 P. M.

N. B. BOYDEN,
REAL ESTATE & GENERAL BROKER,
Room No. 1, 106 Madison St.,   CHICAGO.

Large Lists of City and Country Property always for Sale.

LOANS NEGOTIATED.

ISAAC R. HITT, *late Agent State Bank.*   SETH W. HARDIN, JR., *late Cushman, Hardin & Bro., Bankers.*   WILLIS M. HITT, *late of LaSalle, Ill.*

HITT, HARDIN & HITT,
REAL ESTATE & LOAN AGENCY,
Room No. 10 Tribune Building,
Corner of Madison and Dearborn Sts.,   CHICAGO, ILL.

Loans negotiated and Taxes paid in all the States and Territories.

JAMES R. STANLEY, NOTARY PUBLIC.

ROBERT C. GIVINS.   JAMES H. GILBERT.

GIVINS & GILBERT,
ATTORNEYS-AT-LAW,
Real Estate Dealers and Loan Brokers,

OFFICE:
ROOM 3, TRIBUNE BUILDING,   **CHICAGO.**

JOHN K. WINCHELL,
ARCHITECT,
129 Dearborn St., Rooms 7 & 8,   CHICAGO.

Plans and Specifications for all descriptions of Private and Public Buildings, Stores, Churches, Schools, etc., furnished at low and reasonable rates.

Orders Promptly Attended to.

J. E. BURCHELL.　　　　　　　　　　B. F. JACOBS.
J. E. BURCHELL & CO.
DEALERS IN
Real Estate,
122 WASHINGTON ST.,

Improved and Unimproved City Property,
Suburban Lots, Western Lands, &c.

REFERENCES:—Lunt, Preston & Kean, and Tyler, Ullman & Co., Bankers, J. V. Farwell, Jno. B. Drake, Hon. Samuel Hoard, Chicago; Theo. Polhemus & Co., P. Balen & Co., Phelps, Jewett & Co., New York; Geo. H. Stuart, Philadelphia; Hon. Schuyler Colfax, Washington; M. W. Pond, J. S. Paine, Boston; Gen. J. F. Rathbone, Albany; Second National Bank, Gen. C. B. Fisk, St. Louis; Osgood, Smith & Co., Indianapolis; Wm. Reynolds, A. G. Tyng, Peoria; Col. W. B. Smith, Omaha.

FIRE EXTINGUISHER.
$200,000,000 Worth of Property annually destroyed by Fire in the United States.

The Babcock Extinguisher is offered to the Public as a remedy. Eighty to ninety per cent. of all fires are discovered in their incipiency, but there are no ready means to put them out. Five minutes delay, and the steam fire engines may not control them, and if in season to arrest the flames, the damage by flooding the property with water is often greater than by fire. Two minutes with the Extinguisher, when first discovered, would save all. Delay brings ruin. "Prevention is better than cure."

Always ready! Never fails! Easily carried. *Weighs only 75 pounds filled.* Six Gallons in the Engine charged equal to 450 Gallons common water. Charged in thirty seconds. Can be re-charged in one minute. Throws SIXTY FEET. Puts out burning Kerosene, Benzine, Tar, etc.

Price, $50.00. Charges, 50 Cts. each. Send for Circular.
The Northwestern Fire Extinguisher Co.
F. W. FARWELL, Sec'y, 122 Washington St., Chicago.

F. A. BRAGG & CO.,
REAL ESTATE BROKERS
AND
House Renting Agency.

LOANS NEGOTIATED ON REAL ESTATE SECURITY.

Particular attention given to the Payment of Taxes, Collection of Rents, &c.

129 DEARBORN ST., CHICAGO.

JOS. B. CHANDLER,
Real Estate Broker,
Room No. 9, Speed's Block,
No. 125 DEARBORN STREET,
Between Washington and Madison Sts. - - CHICAGO, ILL.

Large Lists of Improved and Unimproved Property always for sale.
LOANS NEGOTIATED.
Investments made, Titles Examined, Taxes Paid, Rents Collected.

WILLIAM H. RICE.   T. W. WADSWORTH.

RICE & WADSWORTH,
Real Estate Brokers,
87 WASHINGTON STREET,
Rooms No. 1 and 4.   CHICAGO.

MONEY ADVANCED ON GOOD REAL ESTATE SECURITIES.

MAAS & MANZ,
Engravers on Wood,

REYNOLDS' BLOCK,

S. W. Cor. Dearborn and Madison Sts.,   CHICAGO, ILL.

THE
BERLIN
PHOTOGRAPH!

From Re-Touched Negatives,

MADE ONLY AT

CARBUTT'S

PARLOR FLOOR

Photograph Studio,

24 WASHINGTON ST.,

(Next to Wabash Ave.)

Has all the beauty of the Porcelain Miniature, and duplicate copies can be had at same cost of ordinary Photographs.

Operating Hours, from 9 a.m. to 4 p.m.

HALL'S
TINTYPE & FERROTYPE

GALLERY,

122 LAKE STREET,

CHICAGO.

PICTURES OF ALL SIZES

Taken and Finished in a very few minutes.

Small Sizes only Twenty-five cts. per doz.

LARGER, PROPORTIONATELY CHEAP.

Albums, Frames and Cases

ALWAYS ON HAND.

FAIRBANKS'
STANDARD
SCALES!

Nearly 200 Modifications.

Also, Warehouse Trucks, Grain Wagons, Baggage Barrows, Money Drawers, Letter Presses, &c.

WESTERN WAREHOUSES:

FAIRBANKS, GREENLEAF & CO.,

226 and 228 *Lake Street*, CHICAGO.
209 *Market Street, St. Louis.*

Scales Repaired Promptly.

MATHUSHEK
PIANO FORTE CO.,

DEPOT, - - *109 DEARBORN STREET,*

Also, Agency of

PHELPS & GOODMAN'S ORGANS AND MELODEONS.

Special attention invited to the Orchestral (common sized square), and Colibri, "the great soul in a small body." The Patent Linear Bridge gives to these instruments marvelous power and unequaled tone.

The two highest Diplomas and Medals of the Great Fair of the American Institute, Oct., 1867.

Agents throughout the Northwest wanted.

SIDNEY W. SEA,
Gen'l Agent for West and Northwest,
109 Dearborn St,, Chicago, Ill.

G. H. NORRIS & CO.,
REAL ESTATE,

Room 1, U. S. Express Building,

Corner Clark and Lake Streets.
Entrance: 128 LAKE STREET.

AGENTS FOR

PURCHASE AND SALE OF REAL ESTATE,

For Leasing and Collecting Rents in City of Chicago.

ALSO,

DEALERS IN LANDS IN ILLINOIS AND ADJOINING STATES.

Pay Taxes and Investigate Titles.

SAMPSON SCALE CO.

J. S. GRIFFITH & CO.,
N. W. COR. LAKE AND LA SALLE STS., CHICAGO.
General Agents for the Northwest.

D. M. GRAHAM.   J. W. FREE.   D. L. PERRY,
Notary Public.

GRAHAM, PERRY & CO.,

Real Estate

AND

Loan Agents,

Room 8 Major Bl'k, cor. La Salle & Madison St.

CHICAGO.

Parties looking for investments will find on our books a choice list of Business and Residence Property, improved and unimproved, in the city. Some very desirable acre tracts suitable for sub-division, outside old limits.

1,000 LOTS

and 75 Acres, in tracts of from ½ to 10 acres, at Jefferson, only 25 minutes by steam cars, and one hour's drive on good plank road. Payments can be made monthly, quarterly or yearly. Lands and Town Property, improved and unimproved, in all of the Western States, for sale and exchange.

D. WITKOWSKY, Sr.,

A Merchant of prominent standing for twenty-two years in this city, offers to the Public at the

STAR

Clothing Store

AND THE

STAR HAT, CAP AND FUR STORE,

ONE OF THE

Finest and Best Selected Stocks,

That was ever offered before in his line in this Market. He will give his personal attention to his customers. A very fine line of

Gents' Furnishing Goods

May be found at all times in his Stock.
A fine line of

French, Belgian, German, Scotch and West of England

CLOTHS, CASSIMERES, DOESKINS, AND RICH SILK VELVETS,

For the Custom Department,

ALWAYS KEPT ON HAND,

Nos. 64 & 66 Randolph St., and 66, 68 & 70 State St.,

CHICAGO, ILL.

A. J. AVERELL,
G. M. HIGGINSON,
REAL ESTATE BROKERS,

NO. 7 METROPOLITAN BLOCK,

CHICAGO, ILL.

Sell on Commission First Class Business and Residence Property, centrally located, Improved and Unimproved; also Lands by the Acre in the City of Chicago and its Suburbs.

A large list of Valuable Property now for sale, to which the attention of the public is respectfully directed.

G. S. HUBBARD, Jr.   R. N. JACKSON.

HUBBARD & JACKSON,
REAL ESTATE AND LOAN BROKERS,

No. 121 DEARBORN STREET,

CHICAGO.

GEO. W. WAITE & SON,
REAL ESTATE DEALERS,

ROOM 9, TRIBUNE BUILDING,

Corner Madison and Dearborn Streets,

CHICAGO.

THE GREAT
EAST INDIA TEA COMPANY

83 State and 116 Clark Sts.

We Import our own Teas and Coffees,

AND RETAIL THEM AT

NEW YORK CARGO PRICES.

STURGES, McALLISTER & CO.,
Commission Merchants for the Sale of
WOOLEN & COTTON GOODS
AND WOOL,

Nos. 80 and 82 Wabash Ave.,   **CHICAGO.**

A. GOLDSMID.   I. N. MARKS.

A. GOLDSMID & CO.,
Licensed Pawnbrokers
AND DEALERS IN
WATCHES, JEWELRY AND PRECIOUS STONES,
281 South Clark St., Corner Van Buren,

Private entrance on Van Buren;   **CHICAGO.**

Liberal advances made on Merchandise of every description, and Cash paid for old Gold and Silver, Gold Dust, Silver Ore, Old Coins, Curiosities, &c.

Thos. Lord, 52 Cedar St., N. Y.   L. H. Smith, Chicago.
G. W. Stoutenburgh, Chicago.

LORD & SMITH,
Importers and Wholesale Dealers in

Drugs, Medicines,

CHEMICALS,

Perfumery and Toilet Articles,

Patent Medicines, Paints, Oils, Varnishes,

BRUSHES, WINDOW GLASS,

AND

Druggists' Glassware, Dye Stuffs,

And Manufacturers' Stock generally,

86 Wabash Av. and 12 Dearborn Place,

CHICAGO, ILL.

Orders Executed Promptly at lowest Market Prices.

QUALITY OF GOODS GUARANTEED.

Being now well settled in our New Store, No. 86 Wabash Avenue, and having greatly increased facilities of every kind for doing business, we shall make renewed efforts to merit the approbation of all who may favor us with their orders. Our terms are cash, rendering statements on the 20th of each month.

O. R. KEITH. E. G. KEITH.
EDSON KEITH. J. L. WOODWARD.

KEITH BROTHERS,

Manufacturers and Jobbers of

HATS, CAPS

AND FURS,

MILLINERY & STRAW GOODS

Buffalo Robes, Buck Goods, Umbrellas, &c.

68 & 70 Wabash Avenue
And 3 & 4 Dearborn Place,

CHICAGO.

Bowen,

Whitman &

Winslow,

WHOLESALE

DRY GOODS!

15 and 17 Randolph Street.

We Buy and Sell Goods on a Cash Basis, are under light expenses, and are determined our customers shall own their Goods cheaper than those of any other house in the country.

Orders carefully filled at lowest rates.

JAS. W. SCOVILLE.   J. D. HARVEY.

SCOVILLE & HARVEY,

REAL ESTATE

AND LOAN BROKERS,

No. 4 Metropolitan Block,

CHICAGO, - ILLINOIS.

We have for Sale at all times a choice list of

SUBURBAN AND INSIDE PROPERTY,

Loans for Long or Short Time,

NEGOTIATED ON THE MOST FAVORABLE TERMS.

SPECIAL ATTENTION GIVEN TO THE MANAGEMENT OF PROPERTY FOR NON-RESIDENTS.

John V. Farwell & Co.

Wholesale

DRY GOODS!

NOTIONS,

AND WOOLENS,

42, 44 and 46 Wabash Ave.

JOHN V. FARWELL.
CHAS. B. FARWELL.
WM. D. FARWELL.
} **CHICAGO.** { JOHN K. HARMON.
BENJAMIN F. RAY.

We make largest sales, because we sell cheaper than our neighbors.

Orders will receive prompt and careful attention.

We do not interfere with the retailer by retailing ourselves, but are content to sell only at wholesale.

S. H. KERFOOT.   J. F. PIERSON.

Chicago Real Estate Agency
OF
S. H. KERFOOT & CO.,
Established Seventeen Years.

We have, since 1852, been uninterruptedly engaged in the

General Real Estate Agency and Brokerage,
IN THE GROWING CITY OF CHICAGO, ILLINOIS.

We manage Estates and pay Taxes in ILLINOIS, WISCONSIN, IOWA, MINNESOTA, and the North-West generally. We buy and sell Real Estate for residents and non-residents. We have, at our own expense, compiled a most complete ATLAS OF CHICAGO, showing all subdivisions of Lots and Blocks, the sizes and locations of the same, and giving every information regarding Chicago City Real Estate which an Atlas can be made to give. Our Office Real Estate Bulletin always shows a Choice and Desirable *List of Lots, Blocks, Lands, River Fronts, Manufacturing and Business Property, always for Sale.*

To Capitalists seeking investments we offer every inducement to consult our Office, and we pledge ourselves to do our very best to protect their interests.

The Unparalleled Growth of Chicago,

The unquestionable reality of her increase in Commerce, Manufactures, Rail Roads, Grain Trade, Lumber Business, and all lines of traffic, makes the growth certain to continue. The continuance of the growth of Chicago, even at a moderate and healthy pace, makes

Chicago Real Estate Investments better than any Stocks, or Bond and Mortgage.

☞ We do NOT advise buying and selling. We counsel permanent investments. These, when judiciously made, always pay when held for a few years.

We invite correspondence and inquiry, personally or by letter, and will promptly give the information asked.

Our Senior Partner is the President of the Chicago Board of Real Estate Brokers, and its rules govern our office.

REFERENCES.

The Presidents and Cashiers of the First, Second and Third National Banks, Chicago.
Sol. A. Smith, President Merchants' Loan and Trust Co., Chicago.
Hon. Wm. Bross, President Manufacturers' National Bank, Chicago.
The Chicago Commercial Community generally.
Charles MacAlester, Esq., Philadelphia.
William G. Harrison, Esq., Baltimore.
Robert J. Brent, Esq.,   "
Thos. H. Falle, Esq., Water St., cor. of Pine, New York.
John Ferguson, Esq., 85 Pine Street, New York.
Franklin Haven, Esq., Merchants' National Bank, Boston.
Peter Hubbel, Esq., Charlestown and Boston.
John H. Shoenberger, Esq., Pittsburg, Pa.
Hon. Lyman Trumbull, Washington, D. C.
Hon. Norman B. Judd,   "   "
Hon. John F. Farnsworth,   "   "
Hon. Robert C. Schenck,   "   "

Farm and Fruit Lands in the Garden State.

The Illinois Central Railroad Co.
OFFER FOR SALE, IN TRACTS OF 40 ACRES AND UPWARDS,

630,000 ACRES OF LAND,

All lying adjacent to this Railway, and none being farther from it than 15 miles.

For Grain of all Kinds, and Stock-Raising, these lands present unsurpassed advantages. Farmers from Ohio and Indiana, and the more densely-settled portions of older States, are investing in these cheaper lands, which produce with less labor, and in greater abundance, the crops common to all the Northern and Middle States.

Among the most profitable sources of wealth, is that of cattle raising, and the business has become immense. Sheep thrive well, requiring fodder but a short season, and cheese factories are being successfully established along the whole line. Fruit Growing.—The Fruit region of Southern Illinois, for its marvelous fertility, has a national reputation.

These lands are now offered at from $7 to $12 per acre, (with some few tracts at higher figures,) rated according to quality and nearness to stations.

TITLE IN FEE SIMPLE FROM THE STATE.

TERMS OF PAYMENT:—These lands are sold on credit or for cash. A deduction of ten per cent. from the credit price is made to those who purchase for cash.

ALL STATION AGENTS ON THE LINE ARE PROVIDED WITH PLATS, showing the lands for sale in their vicinity. Persons coming through Chicago can call at the office in the Land Department Building, 58 Michigan Avenue, opposite the Great Central Depot, where prices and a pamphlet giving information upon all points will be furnished; or address, by letter, for the same, to

JOHN B. CALHOUN, Land Commissioner,
Illinois Central Railroad Co., CHICAGO, ILL.

www.ingramcontent.com/pod-product-compliance
Lightning Source LLC
Chambersburg PA
CBHW031812230426
43669CB00009B/1113